# Surviving and Prepping with Rice and Beans. 3 Books in 1

LOTS OF TASTY SUPERFOOD SURVIVAL RECIPES,
PREPPER'S WATER SURVIVAL GUIDE,
WATER BATH CANNING & PRESERVING METHODS
TO THRIVE AND LIVE OFF-GRID

Reed Parker

# About the Author

Reed Parker is a man with a simple mission: learn to survive and live. As a married man and father of two, Reed Parker understands how important it is to keep your family and yourself safe. As a citizen of the world, Parker has crossed deserts, forests, and anything in between with the company of his wife. Together, they have learned that being a prepper is more than being prepared, it is soaking in everything that life gives.

During one of their trips to China, they realized that most of their recipes involve rice and beans to some capacity. Noticing that most of the nutrients they require are commonly available worldwide, they decided to try out as many recipes as they could using this staple. The challenge was creating meals that were delicious, easily stored, and could last long after their preparation.

But now the question was, what if we run out of water? Not only should they be prepared beforehand but be ready to quickly gather and search for all of their basic necessities. This leads to the realization that many catastrophes can be avoided with a basic diet, knowledge of your surroundings, and an appetite for learning.

When not travelling, he loves to write and share his passion with the world. A prepper at heart, Reed makes sure that you are prepared even when the unprecedented is knocking at the door.

# About This Bundle

Someone who has made preparations for calamities despite the fact that they may not be totally foreseeable is known as a prepper. Some catastrophes might strike when you are away from home or even in your own house. Preparedness enthusiasts need to be aware of the steps they should take both before and after a natural catastrophe strikes.

At its most basic, "prepping" is a condensed form of the words "preparation" and "preparing," but in today's context, the term "prepping" refers to an entirely other set of activities. Now, the term is often used in conjunction with making preparations for various emergency situations and severe calamities. It begins with the most fundamental preparations, such as storing food, water, and medications, but it quickly expands well beyond that point.

In the end, we want to actually be able to endure any potential tragedies by being well-prepared for them.

**In the first book, you will know about how you can survive with rice and beans.** That, when it comes to emergency preparedness, most people think about canned goods and what they might need for a few days or weeks, but how about an entire month's worth of food with just one simple - and cheap - cooking staple?

Rice will make up the bulk of your preparedness diet. It can be cooked in rice cookers and lasts for up to 30 days.

You should also consider adding beans, nuts and lentils (with their own cooking times) to round out your menu.

In an emergency situation, you will need to actually find a way to eat the meals you have prepared in advance.

Rice cookers are perfect for the job because you can use them to cook mushrooms and other vegetables, on top of rice and beans.

Rice is easy to prepare and you don't have to worry too much about cooking times (although it's important that you cook the right amount). It also offers the added benefit of being so filling.

**The second book will guide you to survive in a disaster by finding, harvesting, purifying, storing endless water.**

Water is one of the essentials of human life, and it is one that many people take for granted. Many people fail to drink enough water when it is readily available, resulting in different symptoms. However, when one is lost in the wilderness, not drinking water can result in your death within three days. Even if you go on a planned hike, there is always a chance that you get turned around and can't find your way back.

Although you may have packed enough water for your planned hike, likely, it will not last long.

You have to be an observant. Because plants and animals will also give you clues as to where you can find water. Many herbivorous animals travel along well-established game trails to get to a water supply, and you can follow fresh tracks to find their water source.

They are an indicator of there still being water. You can dig a hole at the base of their roots then wait until the liquid starts to pool before you collect it.

And lastly, **the last book is pertaining to Water Bath Canning and Preserving Methods to preserve foods, build a pantry, and try to live longer off-grid.**

Because in the event of a major world calamity, it is likely that virtually all commercial canning and food processing plants will cease operation. Without food that has been sealed properly, most foods will be contaminated and go bad within days or a few weeks. But as long as the food is properly canned at normal boiling temperatures, it will maintain its taste and nutritional value for up to two years or more.

This makes it a very good idea to organize your time and produce in an orderly fashion. Practicing canning is similar to the assembly line fashion. For canning to work best, your workspace must really be organized.

The phenomenon of food prepping or getting meals ready beforehand is not new. The trend is actually quite old now and has often been promoted by dietitians and nutritionists for a sustainable and healthy life. However, the reason it has become a regular in the headlines recently is because of everything that has actually been going on in the world right now.

Those people who had been talking about how effective and efficient it is to prepare food and make entire meals to save for later are being appreciated for their organizational skills.

They have been proven right that if a sudden shortage or halt in production arises, we should all have something to fall back on.

With instances where even big supermarkets and stores were stuck due to lack of supply, the preppers who had stockpiled and stored food were in a better position than everyone else.

**You can no longer deny that food prep is done in the right manner, can save lives.** So, what is it actually about? Well, to put it simply, it entails the storing of items and preparing meals that can be portioned out for consumption later.

Once it's prepared, nothing else is required; you can grab it and go whenever you want.

While in the short-term, meal prep is done for about one to two weeks, in some situations, you can also extend the duration to months.

Yes, it is actually possible to save and store meals or food items so that they can be taken out and consumed when there is an emergency.

Now, you might find it difficult to process all this and may be feeling the pressure rising. Well, there is no need to work yourself up into a frenzy. **If you pace yourself and follow a plan, then you will be able to overcome any problem or obstacle.**

# BOOK 1

## SURVIVING AND PREPPING WITH RICE AND BEANS COOKBOOK

# BOOK 2

## PREPPER'S WATER SURVIVAL GUIDE

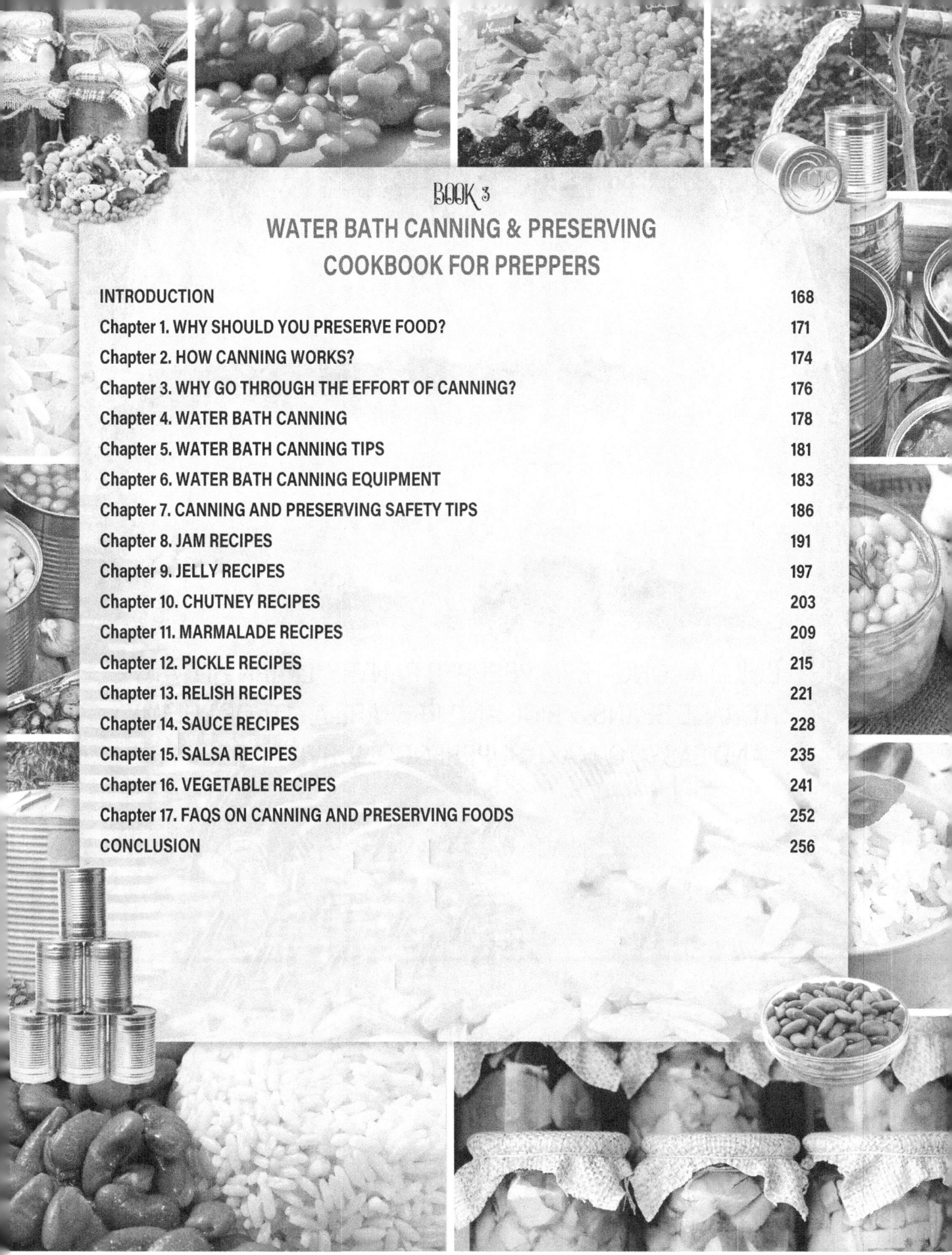

# BOOK 3
# WATER BATH CANNING & PRESERVING
# COOKBOOK FOR PREPPERS

# SURVIVING AND PREPPING WITH RICE AND BEANS COOKBOOK

BUILD A LONG-TERM PREPPER PANTRY, LEARN HOW TO
STORAGE BEANS & RICE AND PREPARE A LOT OF YUMMY
AND EASY-TO-MAKE SUPERFOOD SURVIVAL RECIPES

Reed Parker

# TABLE OF CONTENTS

# INTRODUCTION

The phenomenon of food prepping or getting meals ready beforehand is not new. The trend is actually quite old now and has often been promoted by dietitians and nutritionists for a sustainable and healthy life. However, the reason it has become a regular in the headlines recently is because of everything that has actually been going on in the world right now.

Those people who had been talking about how effective and efficient it is to prepare food and make entire meals to save for later are being appreciated for their organizational skills. They have been proven right that if a sudden shortage or halt in production arises, we should all have something to fall back on.

With instances where even big supermarkets and stores were stuck due to lack of supply, the preppers who had stockpiled and stored food were in a better position than everyone else. You can no longer deny that food prep is done in the right manner, can save lives.

So, what is it actually about? Well, to put it simply, it entails the storing of items and preparing meals that can be portioned out for consumption later. Once it's prepared, nothing else is required; you can grab it and go whenever you want. While in the short-term, meal prep is done for about one to two weeks, in some situations, you can also extend the duration to months. Yes, it is actually possible to save and store meals or food items so that they can be taken out and consumed when there is an emergency.

You might be wondering as to how this all works. Well, it's a combination of factors such as ingredients, cooking, and then storage, which allows the food to retain both its taste and freshness. If you want your food and meal prep to work, you have to first and foremost devise a strategy that employs your survival skills and abilities in the best way possible.

This basically means that you have to think and eliminate all the factors that could result in the failure of the system. Avoiding food items that invite germs, insects or bacteria is one of them. The other is slacking off with meal prep and leaving it to do another time.

# Chapter I.
# Why You Need a Food Storage Pantry

The importance of survival food storage cannot be neglected. No one can survive without a constant supply of food. Living without food and water causes malnutrition, deficiency diseases, and ultimately death. There are certain crisis conditions in which securing a regular supply of food is just not possible. The year 2020 is a recent example of such a crisis. Worldwide lockdowns made it difficult to go out and buy groceries on a weekly basis. Similarly, in other pandemics, war-like conditions, famine, and natural disasters, mankind is met the most difficult circumstances, and such conditions call for food stock that is available at home. This stock must be sufficient enough to meet the needs of every family member as well as ensure good health.

In this chapter, we will actually examine factors that make survival food important. We will learn how haphazard food management results in wasted resources, including the time and effort you put in. According to food science, only a well-planned and well-written food management program can guarantee good health and food security for a longer duration.

Following are some of the known benefits of survival food and its storage.

## Survival During Crisis

Who knows how long a crisis will last? It can take weeks to months, depending on the changing circumstances. You cannot simply rely on external food sources in such changing and ever-wavering conditions. Running out of food and living for days without it is simply not a choice. The only argument that highlights the importance of survival food the most is that our existence depends on it. Now, imagine there is an impending crisis, and you are haphazardly stocking food in your house, and then the food supply is cut off. In a week or two, you will realize that you are running out of some of the basic ingredients needed to cook a complete meal. If only you had prepared a comprehensive list of items along with their required amounts, and then grocery shopped accordingly, such a situation could have been avoided!

Survival is more than living: It is about living a healthy and active life. For such a life, you must have everything healthy to eat. Without sufficient survival food stock at home, you cannot guarantee sound mental and physical health.

## Food Security in Difficult Times

One of the profound reasons that we need to stock survival food at home is food security. It does not even have to be a crisis in order for us to do so. For instance, if you are always working and don't get enough time to consistently buy your groceries, having non-perishable survival food items stocked in your pantry will help big time.

Storing food for a month or more is commonplace in circumstances where there is a constant threat of food shortages or inflation. People then bulk buy the required items and store them in their pantries. Basement storage is also a common practice in places where there are harsh living conditions. People in those places keep their basements filled with survival food items for three to six months, or even for a year. For instance, people living in extremely cold climates stock up on food before winter.

# LEARNING FOOD MANAGEMENT

The best part about survival food storage is that it equips you with all the right skills to manage food. Even on normal days, when we grocery shop and stock our kitchen cabinets with weekly staples, we tend to waste a lot of our energy, time, effort, and money due to our inadequate understanding of food and lack of management skills. But once you go through this whole process of survival food storage, from initial research to list-making, buying in bulk, obtaining appropriate storage items and materials, then packing the food and storing it in an orderly fashion, you become an expert at managing a large amount of food. And not only that, when you live on the survival food, you also learn how to effectively utilize that food without wasting a single bit of it. In order to actually increase the utility of the food, you also improve your cooking skills so that you can actually enjoy a variety of flavors and aromas.

Having these food management and utilization skills can prove to be more helpful on normal days. Now you will be able to buy more food on a smaller budget, and that food will be healthy and nutritious, carefully managed, and stored.

# UNINTERRUPTED SUPPLY OF ENERGY

The concept of survival food revolves around the provision of an adequate amount of energy to the body. In testing times, this food proves to be a constant source of energy for both the mind and the body. The list of the survival food shared in the next chapter rightly indicates that it consists of all those items that are a direct source of carbohydrates, proteins, and fats. The survival food storage techniques further teach how to best use this food to extract an adequate amount of energy per day to meet all the body's needs.

# HELP AND RESCUE

Once the survival food is stocked and packaged in suitable boxes and containers, it gets easier to take with you at the time of need, especially when you cannot leave with all your household items. A survival food package for three to four weeks must be kept ready separately so that you can take it anywhere in difficult circumstances. Whether you are hitchhiking or forest camping, this survival food can help sustain you for days without any fear.

# Chapter 2.
# All About Your Perfect Pantry

Before you start hoarding and stocking food items at home, it is imperative to clearly see the survival food and what it should be like. Understanding the food that you eat and how it stays fresh is the basic science that every prepper must learn in order to manage food over a long period of time. Only this understanding can help you use this food up to its best utility in a crisis.

## Storage-Friendly

It must be light and portable to easily move it around in your pantry and use it whenever needed. Once this food is stored in a plastic bucket, PETE bottles, or other storage pouches, it should take up minimum space so you can store a large amount of food in a smaller space.

For instance, freeze-dried and dehydrated food items are suitable for longer-term storage, but freeze-dried food takes much bigger storage space than dehydrated food. So, the best choice is to store the bulk of dehydrated food instead of freeze-dried food. Dehydrated food can be considered more storage-friendly than freeze-dried food. Such subtle differences can make the food either suitable for storage or non-suitable for longer-term storage. Remember, the whole process should be kept as easy and convenient for you (as the prepper) as possible. You don't need to menu-fatigue yourself during the process.

# Shelf Life

The next important criterion to choosing food for your survival storage is shelf life. It is that time period in which food or any other commodity can be kept or stored without the product losing its original quality and composition. When it comes to food, the shelf life indicates for how long the food is suitable for consumption; beyond the stated shelf life of the food, it can go bad, lose its nutritional value, or turn toxic. Many characteristics determine a food product's shelf life—for example, the content of the food, its sustainability, processing, packaging, and conditions of storage.

# Expiration Dates

We commonly find expiration dates written on the food packaging, but the shelf life is hardly ever mentioned. It is because of the fact that both durations have different significance. The expiration date has importance from the manufacturer's standpoint, whereas shelf life is considered important when the same food is stored. The expiration date is mentioned to mark a time period in which that food must be consumed, and it is determined according to the ingredients and composition of the product, whereas shelf life determines the time period in which food remains to be fit for use. For example, even if pasteurized milk is marked with an expiration date of two weeks, the milk can go bad in just one day once it is opened and placed at room temperature; this means the milk does not have a longer shelf life.

Certain factors determine the shelf life of food, and by controlling these factors, we can extend that amount of time.

# Non-Perishable Food Items

Before marking the survival food as non-perishable, it is important to learn the difference between perishable and non-perishable food. Perishable food items cannot stay fresh for more than a few hours at room temperature, and they can only sustain in low controlled temperatures such as refrigerators and freezers. Even in freezers and refrigerators, such items can only remain fresh for about two or three weeks, depending on their type and composition. For this reason, perishable food is not suitable for survival food storage. You can only store some for immediate and short-term use. Perishable food includes meat, fresh vegetables, fruits, dairy products (such as milk), and cooked food.

These food items do not go bad at room temperature, and they can be cooked easily for a complete meal. Flours, grains, legumes, pasta, whole and powdered spices, etc., are naturally non-perishable. There are some perishable products that can be converted into non-perishable ones through food processing. For instance, fruits like grapes that are otherwise perishable are dehydrated to make raisins that are non-perishable. Similarly, other methods can be employed to expand the fold of non-perishable food items and store them for long durations.

# Cost-Effective

Buying groceries for weekly use is one thing, but to stock them for a month or more can be a big burden on your wallet, and you cannot spend all your money on food when there is a crisis. Therefore, the food we plan to stock for such a condition must also be budget-friendly and cost-effective. It does not have to be cheap and low-quality, but the packaging must be of good quality and reasonable pricing.

There are a few certain ways in which you can buy and store lots of non-perishable food items without feeling a financial burden or strain. First, prepare the list of all the items needed for storage and write down the total amount required. Then divide the total amount into weeks, set a target to buy 25 or 50 percent extra groceries every week, and then stock that extra in your pantry. In this way, your overall financial burden will be divided, and it will take minimum time and effort to stock food on a weekly basis.

# Meals Ready to Eat

While not all survival food items are termed as MREs (meals ready to eat), it is also not a standard food selection standard, but it is important to discuss this concept here, as many preppers commonly use MREs for survival storage. It is mostly utilized by the people who are constantly traveling in a crisis or going to places where there is no food supply. MREs are ready-to-eat meals available in sealed packages. Inside of one is a variety of food items that can provide much-needed calories, carbohydrates, fats, fibers, proteins, etc.

While the idea of having a well processed, healthy, and variety of food in a single package seems tempting, MREs are only suitable for those who cannot manage to stock or who don't have the resources to stock food. These packages are comparatively expensive and will cost you more than the raw non-perishable food. The only advantage these ready-to-eat meals have is that they can be consumed instantly without cooking, and they are rich in nutrients. These packages work well for emergency stockpiling, and for survival food storage, you can buy a few MREs (if affordable) just in case times get really difficult.

# Healthy

Just because there is a crisis and you need to survive for a longer period of time with survival food, it does not mean that you can compromise the quality of the food you're eating. In fact, biological science tells you that the human body needs more calories and nutrients to sustain and live a healthy life in a crisis condition. For this reason, the food that we are storing for such conditions much be rich in nutrients. It must be better in quality than the food we normally eat. There are several perishable food items that we wouldn't be able to consume during the crisis, so the food that we are going to consume must be capable of providing the nutrients of those perishable items as well.

For instance, we cannot consume fresh meat and milk while living on survival food. The protein intake must be met by consuming high protein non-perishable items like grains, legumes, protein powders, dry egg supplements, etc. Similarly, other minerals, vitamins, and fibers widely present in fresh vegetables and fruits must be consumed through canned vegetables, fruits, psyllium husk, whole wheat flour, dried herbs, and dehydrated food products.

# VARIETY

It is natural to get bored and lose your morale during crisis conditions. And if your food is also not attractive, fun, and exciting, you will soon lose your appetite. Indeed, living on survival food is not easy, and it comes with all forms of challenges, but you can turn it around and make things exciting by keeping variety in the stocked food. In fact, most of the food that we can store for this purpose comes in wide varieties, which can store to make a range of different meals. Take legumes, for instance, and you can stock yellow, brown, red, orange, green, and white lentils, then use each to cook various meals. You can use the same lentils for cooking soups, stews, gravies, and snacks.

Having variety in survival food is not an option—it is an absolute need! You can maintain this variety by keeping different seasonings, spices, condiments, a variety of grains, pasta, and beans, etc. By employing different cooking methods, the same food can be cooked repeatedly in different ways. Use slow cooking, stewing, fermentation, baking, or other cooking styles for cooking the basic combination of ingredients. Mix and match one type of seasoning with a different type of grain. Make use of rice and bread to prepare different servings every time. You'll need to be actually as creative as possible in order to keep the menu fun and exciting.

# CHAPTER 3.
# COOKING UNDER CRISIS

When you're in an emergency, your cooking habits might change. Depending on the crisis, different problems could pop up. Maybe your power is out and you can't use your oven and stovetop. Maybe your trips to the grocery store are limited, so you're cooking through your stockpile and need to actually make every meal stretch as much as possible.

## FIRST THINGS FIRST: DO YOU NEED A RATION FOOD?

Depending on the kind of emergency you're dealing with, you may not need to ration food too much. If you're able to access groceries more easily, rationing won't be as much of a concern, but saving money might be. You want to use your stockpile efficiently.

The first thing you actually need to know is that you should not ration water. This is dangerous. Your normal food consumption can be cut down a bit if necessary, but it should be done safely. Food should not be rationed for children or pregnant women. In general, women (who aren't pregnant) need at least 1200 calories a day to maintain their weight while men need at least 1500 calories. If you're active, you'll need more. Stress can also amplify or repress your appetite, so how you feel isn't always a great guideline to follow during tough times. If you know stress tends to trigger overeating and you want to avoid that, you'll need to be more precise about servings.

Nutrition plays a big role, as well. Eating 1200 calories of only pasta is not going to do your body good compared to 1200 calories of pasta, canned meat, and vegetables. In addition to paying attention to calorie count, you want to watch your meal's variety.

Ideally, you want to design your meal plans before an emergency happens. You can just follow your meal plans and recipes, knowing that each serving reflects at least the minimum nutritional and caloric content needed for health.

# Cooking Methods and Supplies

Your normal cooking methods might not be an option during an emergency. If you can't use the microwave, oven, or stovetop, how do you prepare your food? There are a handful of choices:

**Camping stove**

There are tons of camping stoves out there that use a variety of energy sources. Most are reasonably affordable. Fuel sources include propane, butane, and even solar energy. Some types can be used safely indoors, but always check before beginning to cook. Charcoal should never be used indoors. Denatured alcohol stoves are safer indoors than propane or butane. There are also many sizes of camping stoves, which is great if you want a portable cooking source.

**Outdoor grill**

If you have an outdoor grill, you can rely on that to cook just about anything. You can find countless recipes for basically any type of dish for the grill.

### Indoor fireplace

If you actually have a wood-burning fireplace, you can use that to cook. There are grills you can use in the fireplace that make the process easier. Stockpile wood alongside your food supplies if you plan on using your fireplace.

### MRE heater

If you want to save fuel and energy and you have MREs, you can just use an MRE heater for those dishes. These pouches are used by campers and servicemen. They are a combination of powdered food-grade iron, magnesium, salt, and water. When water is poured in the heater pad, it releases enough heat to warm up the MRE in about 12 minutes. These should be used in a well-ventilated area because even though they don't produce carbon monoxide, they can activate detectors. I haven't seen other cooking uses for MRE heaters except for hot drinks like instant coffee or cocoa.

### Traditional wood stove

These stoves are also a heat source that is perfect for cold winters.

### Outdoor fire pit

You can dig a fire pit or buy one that's above ground. There are also different types of fuel you can use, such as propane, natural gas, or wood. Ease of use and price vary depending on the fuel type and other features of the pit.

### Cooking supplies

In addition to the normal pots and pans you most likely also have for cooking, you'll also need firestarters, fuel (wood, propane, butane, etc.), a few can openers, and a cast-iron skillet.

## Cooking Tips

You don't actually need to be a master chef to cook well during stressful times, but here are some tips that can particularly help make the experience easier:

**Don't use more water than you need**

Depending on the emergency, you might want to conserve the water you use for cooking. Most people use too much water when they're boiling food like pasta and rice. You only need enough so the food is just submerged. You can also save water by preparing vegetables using the steam created by cooking potatoes, pasta, rice, etc. Just put a steamer basket on top of the boiling pot. Instead of dumping it down the sink, save it and use it for cooking more pasta, rice, and bread. You can even use it to actually water plants. Throw out reused water that's become very cloudy.

**Use spices**

Don't be afraid to actually use spices in your cooking. Bland food is boring. Certain spices can even help make you feel fuller. Cayenne pepper contains capsaicin, an ingredient that's shown to boost your metabolism and suppress hunger.

**Reduce energy consumption with cold meals if possible**

Not all your food needs to actually be cooked to make a good meal. Vegetables can be mixed for delicious and nutritious salads, while oats can soak overnight in water or milk. Serve canned fruit for dessert instead of baked goods. These cold meals are especially refreshing during the hot summer months.

**Learn how to use your specific equipment and practice meals**

The best cooking tip I can offer is to learn how to use your equipment and make the meals you would serve during an emergency. You can figure out if you like a recipe or adjust it based on your family's tastes. Trying out the equipment now also lets you avoid mistakes during an actual emergency and decide if a particular method works for you. Like rotating your stockpile, using your gear and practicing recipes is an important part of fully preparing for any kind of crisis.

# CHAPTER 4.
# LIST OF ALL FOODS TO HAVE: DURATION AND CONSERVATION

Preppers and people who enjoy stocking up on food and other necessities know that they need to plan for the long-term. In order to actually do this, they will store a variety of supplies in their homes and in their vehicles. However, one area that some people overlook is the foods that last a long time.

With food being very important to survive throughout the apocalypse, you need to control every type of food you have. The following is a list of foods that you need to store separately from others.

## 1. Canned foods:

Several cans are needed to survive the apocalypse. This food will last you a long time, and you can use plastic containers to store water. If plastic containers dry out, they can be put in water for drinking.

### 2. Cereal:

If you have a good stockpile of food, you will need to add in a nice supply of grain and cereal. This is because of the first-class nutrients that cereal will give.

### 3. Rice, Pasta, and other dry foods:

Even though there are some people who don't use these items as much, it's important to know that rice can be used to make other goods. Also, dry pasta can be used to make a tasty sauce. Pasta is also very good for keeping you healthy.

### 4. Soups:

Soups will only last a few months in normal conditions. If you want to keep soups in a cool area, they can last a little longer.

### 5. Canned meats:

You will need several cans of meat to survive. This is because you can put meats in a closet in your room, which will keep the food safe. This is good to know, and your meat products will last long.

### 6. Instant coffee, tea, and milk:

Even though some people may not drink milk with their coffee, there will be no coffee without milk in an apocalypse. Milk is a good resource to use when you're hungry.

### 7. Spices:

In an apocalypse, you will need spices if you want to prevent decay in your food. Spices will last a long time as long as you store them properly.

### 8. Snack foods:

When you're going through a lot of food in daylight, it's wise to look for snacks to eat. These include chips and energy bars. Even the items from gas stations will last a long time.

### 9. Oatmeal and noodles:

On the off chance that you need to leave your shelter due to an emergency, you will need oatmeal and noodles to eat before you leave. This can be good for breakfast time since you can eat enough to feel full.

### 10. Other types of food that are not listed:

If you have a lot of food, be sure to get other food that is not on this list. This is because you may need these types of food to cook or to snack on.

### 11. Root vegetables:

Place the food in a freezer if your root vegetables are starting to rot. This will prevent them from spoiling and getting stale soon after.

### 12. Fresh fruits and vegetables:

Like canned fruits and vegetables, these can last longer by being placed in a freezer. Place them in a freezer when they're starting to become too ripe. This way, you will ensure that the food will last as long as possible.

### 13. Drinkable water:

You need to make sure that you have enough water to drink. Store this in an opaque container because you'll want to see that the container has water. Keep it in a low, safe area with security locks.

# CHAPTER 5.
## BEANS AND RICE, THE BEST SURVIVAL FOOD

Beans and rice, two of the world's most popular staples. Beans provide protein from plants, and rice provides your body with lots of energy. Combined with herbs and spices, beans are a good source of vitamins like folate, thiamin, niacin and riboflavin. They also contain actual important minerals such as iron. The carbs in these legumes give you important energy boosts too!

This book is all about the importance of beans in survival food since they can make any meal more satisfying without having to spend too much time cooking or searching for ingredients that may not be available during an emergency situation. I have worked with beans in cooking over the years, mostly because of the texture and taste they give to stews, soups and other dishes. The ones that I use the most are black beans and kidney beans, but there are many other fantastic ones to choose from. Beans must be soaked before cooking because they contain lectins or proteins that make them harder to digest. A simple way to get rid of these proteins is by soaking them overnight using plenty of water. Also, you should remove the hulls before boiling them for about five hours because these are hard to digest too. The longer you cook the beans, the better the quality of your meal.

Rice is another food that can be prepared in a survival situation because it is commonly available and easy to use. However, it needs to be kept dry because it tends to stick together if it gets wet. It is important to clean the rice before cooking by washing off the impurities and letting it soak overnight because this will give you a better texture in the final dish. You can boil or steam your rice, but I prefer doing both with a pressure cooker as this reduces cooking time.

# BENEFITS

Beans provide fiber and other nutrients important for digestive health while rice is an excellent source of carbohydrates. By combining these two easy-to-find foods into one dish you can create a complete meal full of nutrients that will leave you feeling satisfied and you won't need to prepare anything else on the side. By adding some green vegetables such as broccoli, a small amount of dried or prepared fresh herbs such as parsley, mint, dill or basil and some low-fat cheese, you can really elevate the flavor of a simple rice and beans dish. If you're looking for a healthy and affordable way to pack in the protein, beans and rice are your best bet. Not only do they make a high-quality substitute for meat when you want to cut down on costs, but they also deliver exceptional nutritional value.

Beans are a complete protein source, meaning they offer all nine essential amino acids that our bodies need but can't produce themselves — an amazing feat considering it's usually really hard to find this spectrum of amino acids in plant-based foods! This means beans can give vegetarians an incredibly reliable way of getting their daily protein requirements met without resorting to animal sources.

Brown rice is also a complete protein source and it offers more fiber and B vitamins than white rice. As an added bonus, beans and rice are both very cost effective - especially when purchased in bulk - making them a widely accessible way to actually get the nutrition your body needs.

Now let's look at the ways beans and brown rice can benefit your health:

**High in Fiber**: Both beans and rice offer roughly 6 grams of dietary fiber per cup, which means you're getting a satisfyingly large dose of this important nutrient every time you eat a dish that contains them. Beans are particularly good for fiber intake due to their high fiber content and complex carbs that make it easily digested.

**High in Vitamin E**: Not only do brown rice and beans contain significant levels of beta-carotene, they also boast some impressive levels of vitamin E. Brown rice and beans both have around 9 milligrams of vitamin E per cup, which is pretty "healthy" for a plant-based food!

**Contribute to Healthy Digestion**: Beans are an excellent source of prebiotics. When consumed in the right amount, prebiotics can help stimulate healthy gut function. When prebiotics reach the large intestine, they help facilitate the growth of beneficial bacteria that make for a healthy digestive tract.

**Provide Protein You Need**: Beans and rice are actually a great way to include protein in your diet without resorting to meat or other animal-derived foods, because both are nutrient-dense sources of complete protein (each one contains all 9 essential amino acids).

**An Excellent Alternative to Meat**: Beans and rice have a nice flavor that makes it easy to replace animal protein sources with these more nutritious ingredients. Even better, they're highly affordable ingredients that you can purchase in bulk, which makes them very cost effective.

**Nutritional Information for Beans and Rice**:

- Cooked beans contain about 14 grams of protein per cup.
- 1 cup of cooked beans or ½ cup of raw beans has an excellent source of folate.
- Brown rice is actually an excellent source of magnesium and iron, as well as being a good source of B vitamins.
- Beans and brown rice have a good amount of thiamin and niacin. A cup has about 4 milligrams of thiamin (vitamin B1). Brown rice contains about 4 milligrams niacin (vitamin B3), which is an essential nutrient for the metabolism of fats in the body.
- 1 cup of cooked beans contains about 3 mg of iron, while a cup of brown rice has 1 mg.
- Beans have about 27 mg of magnesium per cup, which is about 9% of the Recommended Daily Allowance for magnesium (400 mg daily). They are a good source of copper and potassium, with 1 cup providing about 8% of the RDA for each one. Potassium is an electrolyte found in plants that allows the muscles to contract and helps control the muscle cells' nerves. Copper is involved in bone health, oxygen transportation and brain function. Beans have also high levels of folate (about 40% RDA).

# Chapter 6.
## Rice and Beans Recipes

## 1. Asian Beans and Rice with Pineapple

**Serving Size: 4**

**Preparation Time: 7 minutes**

**Cooking Time: 43 minutes**

**Ingredients:**

- 2 cups of cooked brown rice
- 1 ½ cups of canned garbanzo beans, rinsed and drained
- ½ pineapple, peeled, cored and sliced
- 1 cup of frozen peas, thawed
- ½ cup of fresh cilantro
- 2 medium carrots, thinly sliced
- 4 cloves of garlic, minced
- 1 lime, halved
- 1 tablespoon of vegetable oil, divided
- 2 teaspoons of grated fresh ginger
- 3 tablespoons of reduced-sodium soy sauce
- fresh cilantro leaves

**Directions:**

- Heat 2 tsps of oil over medium heat in a skillet. Add the pineapple slices and cook for approximately about 2 minutes per side. When the pineapple slices are lightly browned, remove them from the skillet and set aside.
- Add the remaining 1 tsp of oil into the skillet. Add the carrots and cook until tender, for about 5 minutes. Stir in the ginger and garlic and cook for half a minute, until fragrant.

- Mix in the peas, garbanzo beans and brown rice. Cook for about 4 minutes, until heated through, stirring occasionally. Add the cilantro and return the pineapple slices to the skillet and heat through.
- Serve warm with a squeeze of lime. Top with some cilantro leaves.

# 2. Avocado Black Bean Eggs

**Serving Size: 2**

**Preparation Time: 5 minutes**

**Cooking Time: 5 minutes**

**Ingredients:**

- 2 teaspoons of grapeseed oil
- 1 large garlic clove, sliced
- 1 red chili pepper, seeded and thinly sliced
- 2 large eggs
- 1 (14-ounce) can black beans (do not drain); or 5 ounces dry black beans, soaked and cooked
- 1 (14-ounce) can cherry tomatoes
- ¼ teaspoon of cumin seeds
- 1 small avocado, pitted, halved, and sliced
- A handful of cilantro, chopped
- 1 lime, cut into wedges

**Directions:**

- In a large saucepan or skillet, heat the prepared oil over medium heat.
- Add in the garlic and chili pepper. Cook until fragrant and softened.
- On one side of the pan, crack the eggs and cook until they begin to set.
- Add the beans with their juices and stir gently.
- Add the tomatoes and cumin seeds. Cook until beans are warmed through, then remove from the heat.
- On serving plates, arrange the avocado slices and cilantro. Top with the bean mixture. Squeeze the prepared lime wedges on top and serve warm with additional lime wedges, optional.

# 3. Bacon Beans

**Serving Size: 4**

**Preparation Time: 15 minutes**

**Cooking Time: 23 minutes**

**Ingredients:**

- 3 slices of thick cut bacon
- 2 pints of canned green beans

**Directions:**

- Boil green beans in water for 10 minutes, then drain.
- Fry bacon until crispy in a skillet over medium-high heat.
- Remove bacon and reserve about half of the grease.
- Chop bacon finely and return to skillet.
- Add drained beans to skillet and cook for 5 minutes, stirring and tossing.

# 4. Baja Black Beans and Rice with Corn

**Serving Size: 6**

**Preparation Time: 7 minutes**

**Cooking Time: 43 minutes**

**Ingredients:**

- 2 cups of brown rice
- 1 ½ cups of canned corn, drained
- 1 ½ cups of black beans, rinsed and drained
- ½ cup of chopped cilantro
- ½ cup of chopped red onion
- 4 fresh tomatoes, diced
- 1 jalapeño pepper, seeded and diced
- 1 tablespoon of olive oil
- 2 tablespoons of fresh lime juice
- ¼ teaspoon of fresh ground pepper
- ½ teaspoon of salt

**Directions:**

- Place the rice in a saucepan, pour in cold water to cover the rice by a few inches and bring to the boil. Reduce the heat, cover the prepared pot and let it simmer for 20-25 minutes, until the rice is tender.
- In a large-sized bowl, combine all the ingredients and mix well.
- When the rice is done, divide it into plates and top with a big scoop of the black bean mixture.

# 5. Baked Beans

**Serving Size: 6**

**Preparation Time: 8 minutes**

**Cooking Time: 15 minutes**

**Ingredients:**

- 1 pound of dried navy beans
- 2 bay leaves
- 1 cup of onion, chopped finely
- 6 tablespoons of tomato paste
- 3 tablespoons of brown sugar
- 1 ½ tablespoon of Worcestershire sauce
- 1 ½ teaspoon of mustard powder
- 1 ½ teaspoon of salt
- 1 ½ teaspoon of ground black pepper

**Directions:**

- In a Dutch oven, add beans and enough water to cover over high heat and cook until boiling. Remove the pan of beans from heat and set aside, covered for about 1 hour.
- Drain the beans and then add enough fresh water to cover. In the pan of beans, add bay leaves over high heat and cook until boiling. Boil for about 2 minutes. Drain the beans, reserving the cooking liquid.
- For sauce: In a large microwave-safe bowl, add remaining ingredients and stir to combine. Add reserved 3 cups of hot cooking liquid and microwave or about 5 minutes.
- Remove the bowl of sauce from the microwave and mix well. In 3 (1-pint) hot sterilized jars, divide the beans. Fill each jar with hot sauce mixture, leaving 1-inch space from the top.
- Run your knife around the insides of each jar to remove any air bubbles. Clean any trace of food off the rims of jars with a clean, moist kitchen towel.
- Close each jar with a lid and screw on the ring. Carefully place the jars in the prepared pressure canner and process at 10 pounds pressure for about 75 minutes.

- Remove the jars from pressure canner and place onto a wood surface several inches apart to cool completely.
- After cooling with your finger, press the top of each jar's lid to ensure that the seal is tight. Store these canning jars in a cool, dark place.

# 6. Baked Spicy Beans and Egg

**Serving Size: 4**

**Preparation Time: 8 minutes**

**Cooking Time: 35 minutes**

**Ingredients:**

- 1 can of cannellini beans
- 1 can of chopped tomatoes
- 4 large eggs
- 3 cloves of garlic, chopped
- 2 tablespoons of olive oil
- Pinch salt and pepper
- ½ teaspoon of paprika
- ½ teaspoon of coriander leaves and stalks, chopped
- 1 slice toasted bread, sliced into sticks

**Directions:**

- Sauté garlic in olive oil.
- Add beans, chopped tomatoes, and paprika.
- Add eggs and allow the whites to set.
- Once the whites are set, mix it all.
- Finish with chopped coriander and season with the prepared salt and pepper to taste.
- Serve with toasted bread sticks.

# 7. Basil White Bean Dip

**Serving Size: 2 half-pint jars**

**Preparation Time: 10 minutes**

**Cooking Time: 15 minutes**

**Ingredients:**

- 2 tablespoons of lemon juice
- ½ teaspoon of salt
- 1 can of cannellini beans
- ¼ cup of olive oil
- ⅛ teaspoon of pepper
- 1 halved clove garlic
- 1 plum tomato
- ⅔ cup of basil leaves

**Directions:**

- Add lemon juice, cannellini beans, garlic, pepper, and salt in a blender.
- Blend till the beans become coarsely chopped.
- Add oil and mix them.
- Add basil and tomato and mix them well.
- With hot boiling water, sterilize the jars and lids inside the water bath canner. After 5 to 10 minutes, remove them and let them stay warm for packing.
- Transfer the mixture into the jars and leave ½ inch headspace. Tighten the jars with the sterilized lids and put them in the hot water bath canner.
- Ensure to leave an inch of water level at the bottom of the jar. Allow the jars to process in the canner for 35 minutes.
- Remove the tint jars and place them on a towel. Let them rest for at least 12 hours before storing.

# 8. Bean Bolognese

**Serving Size: 4**

**Preparation Time: 6 minutes**

**Cooking Time: 26 minutes**

**Ingredients:**

- 1 can of fava beans, drained
- 1 can of diced tomatoes
- 250 grams of fettuccine, cooked
- 1 small onion, chopped
- 4 cloves of garlic, crushed
- 1 celery stalk, chopped
- 2 tablespoons of olive oil
- 1 bay leaf
- ½ cup of white wine
- 1 cup of parmesan cheese, grated

**Directions:**

- Sauté garlic, onion, and celery in oil. Add tomatoes and bay leaf and allow to simmer for a couple of minutes.
- Add beans and white wine to the sauce. Cook until it thickens.
- Pour sauce over fettuccine and top with parmesan cheese before serving.

# 9. Bean, Cheese and Ham Frittata

**Serving Size: 4**

**Preparation Time: 8 minutes**

**Cooking Time: 40 minutes**

**Ingredients:**

- 1 can of green beans, drained
- 1 white onion, chopped
- 4 slices of deli ham, sliced into thin strips
- 4 large eggs
- 2 tablespoons of olive oil
- 1 cup of cream cheese, cubed
- Salt and pepper

**Directions:**

- Sauté white onion in olive oil until soft.
- Add green beans and deli ham in a bowl, whisk eggs, cheese and season with the prepared salt and pepper to taste.
- Add eggs to pan. Make sure that the mixture is distributed evenly.
- Allow to cook until edges set.
- Transfer the pan to oven and bake the frittata for 25 minutes, or until the center sets.
- Cut into 4 wedges before serving.

# 10. Beef, Bean and Barley Soup

**Serving Size: 4**

**Preparation Time: 8 minutes**

**Cooking Time: 40 minutes**

**Ingredients:**

- 2 tablespoons of coconut or olive oil
- 3 cups of freeze-dried diced beef, reconstituted
- ½ cup of dehydrated chopped onion
- 2 teaspoons of minced dehydrated garlic
- ½ cup of dehydrated or freeze-dried chopped celery
- 5 cups of beef or chicken broth
- 6 cups of water
- 1 cup of freeze-dried sliced or chopped carrots
- ½ teaspoon of dry oregano
- ½ cup of dry lentils, rinsed and debris removed
- 1 cup of barley, uncooked
- 1 teaspoon of salt, more to taste
- ¼ teaspoon of ground black pepper

**Directions:**

- Reconstitute onions, garlic, and celery.
- Drain excess water.
- In a prepared large soup pot, heat oil on low heat.
- Add onions, garlic, celery, and beef and cook for about 5 minutes or until meat is lightly browned.
- Add the rest of the ingredients and bring to a boil.
- Lower heat and simmer at a low boil for 1-2 hours.

# 11. Black Bean and Corn Salsa

**Serving Size: 5**

**Preparation Time: 7 minutes**

**Cooking Time: 1 hour 5 minutes**

**Ingredients:**

- 1 pound of dried black beans
- 8 cups of corn
- 2 cups of chopped tomatoes
- 2 onions
- 6 chopped bell peppers
- 3 chopped hot peppers
- 2 tablespoons of red pepper flakes
- 1 cup of chopped cilantro
- 1 tablespoon of ground cumin
- ¼ cup of lime juice

**Directions:**

- Soak the beans overnight in warm water. The following day, drain and rinse them.
- Pour with the beans enough water to cover them. Boil for 35 Minutes while stirring frequently and then drain.
- Place the beans back in the pot along with the corn, tomatoes, onions, peppers, red pepper flakes, cilantro, cumin, and lime juice. Add enough water until the water is one inch above the mixture.
- Let the vegetables come to a boil while stirring frequently. Boil for 10 minutes. Pour the hot vegetables and beans into sterile jars.
- Add enough liquid to cover the vegetables while leaving 1-inch headspace. Wipe the rims clean and adjust all lids. Process for 75 minutes in the pressure canner at 10 pounds for a canner with a heavy gauge or 11 pounds if the pressure canner has a dial gauge.

## 12. Black Bean Quesadillas

**Serving Size: 4**

**Preparation Time: 7 minutes**

**Cooking Time: 43 minutes**

### Ingredients:

- 2 teaspoons of olive oil
- 3 tablespoons of finely diced white onion
- 1 pint of drained black beans
- 1 pint of corn
- 8 ounces of whipped cream cheese
- ½ cup of salsa
- 2 tablespoons of butter
- 8 (8 inch) corn tortillas
- 1 ½ cups of shredded Mexican four cheese blend
- sour cream to taste

### Directions:

- Sauté the onion in olive oil until softened.
- Add the beans, corn, cream cheese and salsa into the skillet stir until well mixed and heated through.
- In a second skillet, melt the butter.
- Place one tortilla in the skillet, spread evenly with cheese.
- Add a scoop of the bean mixture 6. Place a second tortilla on top and cook until bottom tortilla is slightly browned.
- Flip the tortilla in the pan and cook until the other side is lightly browned. Set aside on a plate.
- Repeat with the rest of the tortillas, adding more butter to the pan as needed.
- Serve garnished with sour cream.

# 13. Black Eyed Peas

**Serving Size: 4**

**Preparation Time: 5 minutes**

**Cooking Time: 1 hour 15 minutes**

**Ingredients:**

- 1 ½ pounds of dried black-eyed peas
- 6 tablespoons of chopped onions
- 30 peppercorns
- ¾ teaspoon of dried herbs of your choice
- 1 teaspoon of salt

**Directions:**

- Rinse and soak peas overnight.
- Add rinsed beans to a large saucepot and cover with fresh water. Allow it to boil for 30 minutes.
- Pack beans into each canning jar, distribute all ingredients evenly and add boiling water. Remember to leave a one-inch headspace. Use a spatula to remove air bubbles, then use a clean cloth to wipe jar rims. After that, adjust lids and screw band.
- Set your filled jars in the pressure canner at 11 pounds for dial-gauge or 10 pounds for the weighted canner. Process heat jars for 75 minutes, adjusting for altitude. Switch off the heat and let the pressure drop naturally. Remove the cover lid and allow the jars to cool in the canner for 5 minutes. Take out the jars and cool further. Inspect lid seals after 24 hours.

# 14. Canned Garlic Beans

**Serving Size: 3 jars**

**Preparation Time: 45 minutes**

**Cooking Time: 35 minutes**

**Ingredients:**

- 2 ¼ pounds of dried black beans
- Pinch salt
- 1 cup of water
- a handful of cilantro
- 5 garlic cloves, diced

**Directions:**

- Sort the beans to remove any unwanted particles.
- Place the prepared beans in a large pan and cover them in water, about 2 inches.
- Place the pan on the heat and bring the water and beans to boil for 2 minutes.
- Remove the beans from heat and let soak covered for 1 hour. Drain the water and return the pan back on the heat.
- Add more water until just covered. Add cilantro and garlic. Bring the beans and water to boil for 30 minutes.
- Use a slotted spoon to pack the beans in jars leaving 1-inch headspace. Add ½ tablespoon of salt to each jar then add the cooking liquid to cover the beans.
- Remove the bubbles, wipe the jar rims, place the lids and rings on, and use hands to tighten.
- Process the jars for 60 minutes at 10 pounds pressure. Wait for the canner to depressurize before removing the jars and storing them.

# 15. Chili-Lime Roasted Chickpeas

**Serving Size: 1 half-pint jar**

**Preparation Time: 8 minutes**

**Cooking Time: 55 minutes**

**Ingredients:**

- 1 tablespoon of chili powder
- 2 cans of chickpeas
- 2 tablespoons of ground cumin
- 2 tablespoons of extra virgin olive oil
- 1 tablespoon of lime juice
- 1 teaspoon of grated lime zest
- ¾ teaspoon of sea salt

**Directions:**

- Preheat the oven to 400°F. Spread the chickpeas on foil paper and bake for 45 mins until crunchy.
- Mix all the remaining ingredients. Let chickpeas cool down, then add them to the mixture.
- With hot boiling water, sterilize the jars and lids inside of the water bath canner. After 5 to 10 minutes, remove them and allow them to stay warm for packing.
- Transfer the mixture into the jars and leave ½ inch headspace. Tighten the jars with the sterilized lids and put them in the hot water bath canner. Ensure leaving an inch of water level at the bottom of the jar. Allow the jars to process in the canner for 35 minutes.
- Remove the tint jars and place them on a towel. Let them rest for at least 12 hours before storing.

# 16. Cranberry Beans

**Serving Size: 4**

**Preparation Time: 5 minutes**

**Cooking Time: 55 minutes**

**Ingredients:**

- 2 pounds of shelled cranberry beans
- 3 chopped garlic cloves
- ¾ cup of white wine
- 4 tablespoons of lemon juice
- 6 tablespoons of olive oil
- 6 teaspoons of fresh marjoram
- ½ teaspoon of black pepper
- ¾ teaspoon of salt
- 2 cups of chicken stock

**Directions:**

- In a large container, combine the beans with all ingredients except the chicken stock.
- Pack beans into each canning jar and add chicken broth. Remember to leave a one-inch headspace. Use a spatula to remove air bubbles, then use a clean cloth to wipe jar rims. After that, adjust lids and screw band.
- Set your filled jars in the pressure canner at 11 pounds for dial-gauge or 10 pounds for the weighted canner. Process heat jars for 60 minutes, adjusting for altitude. Switch off the heat and let the pressure drop naturally. Remove the cover lid and allow the jars to cool in the canner for 5 minutes. Take out the jars and cool further. Inspect lid seals after 24 hours.

# 17. Creole Beans and Rice

**Serving Size: 6**

**Preparation Time: 7 minutes**

**Cooking Time: 43 minutes**

**Ingredients:**

- 1 cup of jasmine rice
- 1 ½ cups of vegetable broth
- 1 ½ cups of canned red beans, drained and rinsed well
- 1 white onion, chopped
- 2 stalks of celery, diced
- 1 red or yellow bell pepper, seeded and diced
- 3 cloves of garlic, minced
- 3 cups of frozen sliced okra
- 1 tablespoon of avocado oil
- 1 teaspoon of crushed dried thyme
- 1 teaspoon of paprika
- 1 teaspoon of crushed dried oregano
- ¼ - ½ teaspoon of cayenne pepper
- 1 teaspoon of salt
- ½ teaspoon of ground black pepper

**Directions:**

- Pour the vegetable broth and rice in a medium saucepan and bring to the boil. Cover the pan, reduce the heat and simmer for 15 minutes. Remove from the stove and keep covered for 10 minutes.
- In a large-sized skillet, heat the oil over medium-high heat. Add the celery and onions and cook until the onions become translucent. Add the okra, beans, bell pepper and spices and cook for about 15 minutes. Stir in the garlic and rice. Mix well to coat the rice with all the spices.
- Serve warm.

# 18. Crispy Green Beans Fry with Eggs

**Serving Size: 4**

**Preparation Time: 8 minutes**

**Cooking Time: 35 minutes**

**Ingredients:**

- 1 can of green beans, drained
- 3 medium sized potatoes, diced
- 4 large eggs
- 2 tablespoons of extra virgin olive oil
- 2 cloves of garlic, crushed
- 1 tablespoon of chili flakes
- A pinch of salt and pepper
- 1 teaspoon of paprika

**Directions:**

- Heat oil and fry diced potatoes in garlic until it gets crispy.
- Add green beans and chili flakes.
- Crack eggs into the vegetables and cover the pan.
- Wait until whites are set and season with salt, pepper, and paprika to taste before serving.

# 19. Curried Bean and Rice

**Serving Size: 4**

**Preparation Time: 7 minutes**

**Cooking Time: 29 minutes**

**Ingredients:**

- 1 can of brown lentils, drained
- 3 cups of basmati rice, cooked
- 4 cloves of garlic, crushed
- 2 tablespoons of olive oil
- 1 teaspoon of fresh ginger paste
- 2 teaspoons of red curry paste

**Directions:**

- Sauté ginger and garlic in oil.
- Add curry paste and cook until fragrant.
- Add brown lentils and rice, and mix well.

# 20. Curried Lentils and Rice

**Serving Size: 4**

**Preparation Time: 8 minutes**

**Cooking Time: 35 minutes**

**Ingredients:**

- 1 pound of uncooked lentils, rinsed and soaked if desired
- 8 cups of water, more as needed
- 3 ½ quarts (14 cups) vegetable or chicken broth, divided
- ¾ cup of diced dehydrated onions
- 1 ½ cups of freeze-dried carrot dices
- 2 cans of petite diced tomatoes, undrained
- 1 ½ teaspoon of dehydrated minced garlic
- 1 teaspoon of salt, more to taste
- 1 ½ cups of canned evaporated milk (or ¾ cup of powdered milk mixed with 1 ½ cups of water)
- ⅓ cup of sour cream powder
- 1 tablespoon of curry powder, more to taste
- hot cooked rice

**Directions:**

- Add the lentils, water, and 6 cups broth to a large stock pot (liquid should just cover beans). Bring to a very hot boil, then lower heat to medium.
- Simmer 35 minutes to 1 hour, adding more liquid if needed. Add the rest of the broth (8 cups or 2 quarts), vegetables, garlic, and curry and stir well.
- Allow to cook until vegetables are tender and the liquid is reduced. Before serving, add milk and sour cream powder and mix well using a whisk. Add more curry and salt as desired.
- Serve over hot, cooked rice.

# 21. Eastern Rice and Beans

**Serving Size: 4**

**Preparation Time: 7 minutes**

**Cooking Time: 43 minutes**

**Ingredients:**

- 1 ½ cups of black beans, drained and rinsed
- 1 ½ cups of chickpeas (garbanzo beans), drained and rinsed
- 1 cup of white rice
- 2 ½ cups of vegetable broth
- 1 clove of garlic, minced
- 1 tablespoon of olive oil
- ⅛ teaspoon of ground cayenne pepper
- 2 teaspoons of ground coriander
- 2 teaspoons of ground cumin
- ½ teaspoon of curry powder
- 1 teaspoon of ground turmeric
- salt to taste
- pepper to taste
- naan or flatbread

**Directions:**

- Heat the prepared olive oil in a prepared large skillet over medium heat. Add the garlic and sauté for approximately about 1 minute. Add the rice, stir well and add all the spices and cook for about 5 minutes.
- Pour in the vegetable broth and bring it to a boil. Reduce the heat, cover the skillet and let the mixture simmer for 20 minutes.
- Add the black beans and garbanzo beans and stir gently.
- Serve warm over flatbread or naan.

## 22. FERMENTED BLACK BEANS

**Serving Size: 2**

**Preparation Time: 15 minutes**

**Cooking Time: 55 minutes**

**Ingredients:**

- ⅔ cup of dry black beans
- Filtered water
- 1 tablespoons of whey
- 1 ½ teaspoon of non-iodized sea salt

**Directions:**

- In a prepared large pot of boiling salted water, cook the beans on high for 15 minutes. Cover the large-sized pot, reduce the heat and let the prepared beans simmer for 1 hour. Remove the pot from the heat.
- Once the beans are cool, place them in a large glass jar. Add the salt, the whey and enough of the water to cover the beans. Leave actually at least an inch of head space between the prepared water and the top of the jar.
- Seal the jar and put it in a warm dark place. After 2 days, drain and store in the refrigerator.

## 23. Fermented Pinto Beans

**Serving Size: 2**

**Preparation Time: 15 minutes**

**Cooking Time: 55 minutes**

**Ingredients:**

- 3 cups of pinto beans, cooked and drained
- 1 onion, chopped
- 4 garlic cloves, minced
- 1 tablespoon of non-iodized sea salt
- 4 tablespoons of whey

**Directions:**

- Put the pinto beans, onion, garlic, salt and whey in a bowl and stir with a spoon until combined. Press the beans and ingredients together slightly with the fork. Do not mash the ingredients, but gently tear some of the skin of the beans and mash the onion pieces so they become a little moist.
- Pour this mixture into a quart glass jar. Leave a one inch of head space at the top and put the lid on. Set the jar in a warm place to ferment for 3 days.

## 24. Greek Lentils and Rice

**Serving Size: 4**

**Preparation Time: 7 minutes**

**Cooking Time: 55 minutes**

**Ingredients:**

- ⅓ cup of white rice
- 1 cup of dried lentils
- 1 clove of garlic, minced
- 1 onion, minced
- 1 tablespoon of tomato paste
- 4 tablespoons of olive oil
- salt to taste
- pepper to taste

**Directions:**

- Place the lentils in a pot with plenty of water and bring to the boil. Reduce the heat and cook until the lentils are tender. Drain well.
- In a saucepan, heat the prepared olive oil over medium heat, add the prepared onion and garlic and sauté until translucent. Stir in the rice and cooked lentils. Pour in 2 cups of water. Season to taste and add the tomato paste. Cook for 40-50 minutes.
- Serve warm.

# 25. GREEN BEANS AND RICE WITH PUMPKIN

**Serving Size: 4**

**Preparation Time: 7 minutes**

**Cooking Time: 43 minutes**

**Ingredients:**

- 1 ½ cups of white long-grain rice
- 4 cups of vegetable stock
- ¾ cup of green beans, topped, cut into 2-inch pieces
- 2 cups of butternut pumpkin, deseeded, peeled, cut into 1-inch pieces
- ¼ cup of pine nuts
- 1 red onion, halved, thinly sliced
- ¼ cup of fresh continental parsley leaves
- 1 teaspoon of ground cumin
- 1 tablespoon of olive oil

**Directions:**

- In a large saucepan, combine the vegetable stock, rice, pumpkin and cumin and bring to the boil. Cover the prepared pan, reduce the heat and cook for approximately about 12 minutes, or until the pumpkin and rice are tender.
- Two minutes before the end of cooking, add the beans. Remove from the actual heat and let it sit covered for approximately about 5 minutes.
- Heat a frying pan over medium-high heat. Add the pine nuts and toast them for two minutes, stirring. When toasted, transfer them to a bowl.
- In the same pan, heat the oil over medium heat. Add the prepared onion and cook for approximately about 5 minutes, stirring occasionally, until browned. Remove from the heat.
- Spoon the rice and pumpkin mixture into serving bowl. Sprinkle with toasted nuts and top with the onions and parsley.

# 26. Ham and Mixed Bean Soup

**Serving Size: 4**

**Preparation Time: 7 minutes**

**Cooking Time: 55 minutes**

**Ingredients:**

- 1 (15 ounce) can each of white beans, pintos, and black beans, drained
- 2 quarts (8 cups) water
- 1 cup of dehydrated chopped onion
- ½ cup of chopped dehydrated or freeze-dried celery
- 1 cup of cooked canned ham
- ½ teaspoon of dried oregano
- ½ teaspoon of dried basil
- 2 bay leaves
- 2 cups of freeze-dried carrots, reconstituted
- 1 tablespoon of dehydrated minced garlic
- ½ teaspoon of salt, more to taste
- ground black pepper to taste

**Directions:**

- Add all ingredients to large stock pot.
- Bring to boil initially, then cover and simmer on low to medium for 2-3 hours, making sure not to let it boil over.
- Add more water as needed.
- Remove bay leaves before serving.

# 27. Hearty White Bean Soup

**Serving Size: 4**

**Preparation Time: 7 minutes**

**Cooking Time: 10 minutes**

**Ingredients:**

- 1 can of cannellini beans, drained
- 1 can of tomato chunks
- 5 cups of vegetable stock
- 1 small onion, chopped
- 2 garlic cloves, minced
- 1 stalk celery, sliced
- 2 carrots, cubed
- 2 tablespoons of olive oil
- 1 tablespoon of sage, chopped
- 2 teaspoons of dried oregano
- Salt and pepper

**Directions:**

- Sauté onion, celery, and garlic in olive oil. Add dried oregano, sage, and tomato chunks. Cook until soup simmers.
- Add cannellini beans, carrots, and vegetable stock, and cook until the carrots are soft. Stir occasionally.
- Season with prepared salt and pepper to taste before serving.

# 23. Jamaican Beans and Rice

**Serving Size: 10**

**Preparation Time: 5 minutes**

**Cooking Time: 22 minutes**

**Ingredients:**

- 1 ½ cups of canned red kidney beans, rinsed and drained
- ¼ cup of minced onion
- 2 tablespoons of Olive oil
- 2 cups of long-grain rice
- 2 ¼ cups of water
- 1 ¾ cups of coconut milk
- 1 scallion, chopped
- 1 clove of garlic, crushed
- 1 sprig of fresh thyme
- 1 teaspoon of coconut oil
- 1 whole scotch bonnet hot pepper, not chopped
- salt to taste
- ground pepper to taste

**Directions:**

- Heat the olive oil in a medium-size saucepan over medium heat. Add the scallion, onion, garlic and thyme. Sauté for approximately about a few minutes, until the onions are translucent and lightly browned.
- Stir in the rice and beans. Pour in the coconut milk and water and season with salt and pepper. Add the whole scotch bonnet pepper, stir to combine and bring to the boil.
- When it starts boiling, remove the pepper and cook until the rice is tender and almost all the liquid has been absorbed.
- Cover the saucepan, reduce the heat and let it simmer for approximately about 25 minutes. Remove the large-sized saucepan from the heat and let it actually rest covered for approximately about 10 minutes, so that the steam will finish cooking the rice. Serve hot.

# 29. Kidney Beans Chili

**Serving Size: 18**

**Preparation Time: 15 minutes**

**Cooking Time: 40 minutes**

**Ingredients:**

- 3 cups of dried red kidney beans, soaked overnight and drained
- 1 tablespoon of salt
- 2 cups of onion, chopped
- 1 cup of sweet bell pepper, seeded & chopped
- 6 garlic cloves, minced
- ¼ cup of fresh parsley, minced
- 8 cups of tomato juice
- ½ cup of tomato paste
- 3 tablespoons of red chili powder
- 1 teaspoon of ground black pepper
- 2 teaspoons of dried thyme
- 2 teaspoons of ground cumin

**Directions:**

- In a Dutch oven, add beans and enough water to cover over high heat and cook until boiling. Reduce the heat to a heat of low and cook for about 30 minutes. Drain the beans well.
- For sauce: In a saucepan, add remaining ingredients over medium heat and cook until boiling. Stir in the cooked beans and cook until boiling.
- In 9 (1-pint) hot sterilized jars, divide the beans. Fill each jar with hot sauce mixture, leaving 1-inch space from the top.
- Run your knife around the insides of each jar to remove any air bubbles. Wipe any trace of food off the rims of jars with a clean, moist kitchen towel.
- Close each jar with a lid and screw on the ring. Carefully place the jars in the prepared pressure canner and process at 10 pounds pressure for about 75 minutes.

- Remove the jars from pressure canner and place onto a wood surface several inches apart to cool completely.
- After cooling with your finger, press the top of each jar's lid to ensure that the seal is tight. Store these canning jars in a cool, dark place.

# 30. Lentil and Rice Risotto

**Serving Size: 4**

**Preparation Time: 7 minutes**

**Cooking Time: 33 minutes**

**Ingredients:**

- 2 cups of cooked lentils
- 2 tablespoons of taco seasoning mix
- ¼ cup of water
- 8 large soft tortillas
- 2-3 cups of shredded cheese of choice
- 1 jar of salsa of choice
- 2 cups of rice

**Directions:**

- In a large skillet, heat lentils on low-to-medium heat. Add taco seasoning and water and incorporate them into lentils. Simmer for about 5 minutes until the mixture heats through and thickens.
- Top each tortilla evenly with the lentil mixture and top with rice, salsa, and cheese. Fold into a burrito. Heat in the oven if desired (350 degrees for approximately 10 minutes). Serve with more salsa if desired.

# 31. Mac and Black Bean Casserole

**Serving Size: 4**

**Preparation Time: 8 minutes**

**Cooking Time: 35 minutes**

**Ingredients:**

- 2 ½ cups of water
- ¼ teaspoon of salt, more to taste
- 1 cup of uncooked macaroni
- ¾ cup of reconstituted shredded cheddar cheese
- ¼ teaspoon of ground black pepper
- 1 cup of cooked black beans, drained
- ½ teaspoon of ground cumin
- ¼ cup of milk (mixed from dry)

**Directions:**

- Place water and salt in a medium-sized pan. Bring water to a boil. Add macaroni and turn down the heat. Cook for 2-5 minutes or until desired doneness.
- Drain water. Add cheese and incorporate. Cover to let the cheese melt for 5 minutes. Uncover and add the rest of the ingredients. Mix together and reheat.

# 32. MARINATED FAVA BEANS

**Serving Size: 2**

**Preparation Time: 15 minutes**

**Cooking Time: 25 minutes**

**Ingredients:**

- 1 ½  pounds of fava beans
- 2 tablespoons of red wine vinegar
- ¼ teaspoon of black pepper, ground
- ½ teaspoon of kosher salt
- 2 sprigs of fresh rosemary
- 1 teaspoon of fresh and minced garlic
- 2 tablespoons of olive oil

**Directions:**

- Boil salted water. While water is heating up, remove beans from their pods. Once water is boiling add beans, and cook for about 3 minutes or until tender and green.
- Drain the beans and rinse them under cold water. Pop the fava beans out of their casings and set them aside.
- Mix the vinegar, garlic, olive oil, rosemary sprigs, salt and pepper in a mason jar. Place lid on jar and shake contents to combine. Add fava beans to jar and secure lid. These marinated beans will keep up to three days in the fridge. Allow the beans to actually soak for at least 15 minutes in the mix before serving them.

# 33. Mushroom and Bean Cream Soup

**Serving Size: 4**

**Preparation Time: 7 minutes**

**Cooking Time: 33 minutes**

**Ingredients:**

- 1 can of white beans, drained
- 1 can of mushrooms, drained and chopped
- 4 cups of vegetable stock
- 1 small onion, chopped
- 2 cloves of garlic, minced
- 1 teaspoon of dried basil
- 1 tablespoon of olive oil
- 1 tablespoon of butter
- 1 tablespoon of flour
- ½ cup of cream
- Salt and pepper

**Directions:**

- Sauté onion and garlic in olive oil.
- Add mushrooms and cook until garlic turns golden.
- Add flour. Make sure that it coats the mushrooms.
- Add butter, beans, dried basil, and vegetable stock. Bring to a simmer.
- Turn off heat and stir in cream.
- Season with prepared salt and pepper to taste before serving.

# 34. Pinto Beans Chili

**Serving Size: 18**

**Preparation Time: 15 minutes**

**Cooking Time: 40 minutes**

**Ingredients:**

- 2 pounds of dry pinto beans, rinsed and drained
- 3–4 bay leaves
- Salt, as needed
- 1 tablespoon of olive oil
- 2 onions, chopped
- 2 (28-ounce) cans of petite diced tomatoes
- 1 (15-ounce) can of tomato sauce
- 2 cups of beef broth
- 3 tablespoons of chili powder
- 2 tablespoons of ground cumin
- 2 teaspoons of garlic powder
- 1 teaspoon of dried oregano
- 1 teaspoon of dried thyme
- Ground black pepper, as needed

**Directions:**

- In a large stockpot of water, add beans, bay leaves, 1 tablespoon of salt over high heat and cook until boiling. Reduce the heat to a heat of low and cook for about 30–35 minutes.  Meanwhile, heat oil in a frying pan over medium heat and sauté the onion for about 4–5 minutes. Drain the beans and return to the same pot.
- In the pot of beans, add the cooked onion and remaining ingredients and stir to combine. Put the pan over high heat and bring to a boil.
- In 9 (1-pint) hot sterilized jars, divide the chili, leaving 1-inch space from the top. Run your knife around the insides of each jar to remove any air bubbles.
- Clean any trace of food off the rims of jars with a clean, moist kitchen towel. Close each jar with a lid and screw on the ring.

- Carefully place the jars in the prepared pressure canner and process at 10 pounds pressure for about 90 minutes.
- Remove the jars from pressure canner and place onto a wood surface several inches apart to cool completely.
- After cooling with your finger, press the top of each jar's lid to ensure that the seal is tight. Store these canning jars in a cool, dark place.

# 35. Polenta, Bean and Sausage Casserole

**Serving Size: 4**

**Preparation Time: 5 minutes**

**Cooking Time: 55 minutes**

**Ingredients:**

- 1 ¼ cups of reconstituted freeze-dried sausage crumbles
- 1 cup of dehydrated chopped onions
- 2 tablespoons of reconstituted freeze-dried bell pepper dice
- 4 ½ cups of reconstituted instant dry milk
- 1 ½ cups of reconstituted freeze-dried cheese, divided in half
- ½ cup of freeze-dried scrambled eggs, reconstituted
- 2 teaspoons of dehydrated minced garlic
- ⅔ cup of polenta or coarse cornmeal
- ¾ teaspoon of salt
- 1 teaspoon of dry ground thyme
- 2 teaspoons of olive oil

**Directions:**

- Reconstitute the first six ingredients; drain well.
- Preheat oven to 425°F.
- Allow cooking until thickened, whisking often.
- While cooking cornmeal, heat oil in a large skillet over low-to-medium heat, add sausage, onions, thyme, garlic, and bell pepper, and mix well.
- Once the cornmeal mixture is thickened, remove it eventually from the heat and stir in half the cheese. Mix and cover to allow the cheese to melt.
- Combine all ingredients together. Then add to a 2-quart baking dish.
- Bake for 30-35 minutes or until set. Sprinkle with cheese and cook for 5 minutes more until cheese is melted.

# 36. RED LENTILS

**Serving Size: 8**

**Preparation Time: 8 minutes**

**Cooking Time: 10 minutes**

**Ingredients:**

- 2 cups of red lentils, rinsed
- 4 cups of chicken broth
- 2 small brown onions, chopped finely

**Directions:**

- In a Dutch oven, add lentils, onion, and broth over high heat and cook until boiling. Now set the heat to low and cook for about 5 minutes.
- In 4 (1-pint) hot sterilized jars, divide the lentils. Fill each jar with hot cooking liquid, leaving 1-inch space from the top.
- Run your knife around the insides of each jar to remove any air bubbles. Clean any trace of food off the rims of jars with a clean, moist kitchen towel.
- Close each jar with a lid and screw on the ring. Carefully place the jars in the prepared pressure canner and process at 10 pounds pressure for about 75 minutes.
- Remove the jars from pressure canner and place onto a wood surface several inches apart to cool completely.
- After cooling with your finger, press the top of each jar's lid to ensure that the seal is tight. Store these canning jars in a cool, dark place.

# 37. Rice and Bean Casserole

**Serving Size: 6**

**Preparation Time: 7 minutes**

**Cooking Time: 43 minutes**

**Ingredients:**

- 1 ½ cups of brown rice
- 1 ½ cups (or 1 can) small red kidney beans
- 3 cups of vegetable broth
- 1 ¾ cups of canned organic tomato sauce
- 1 small white onion, finely chopped
- 2 cups of frozen corn
- 2-3 handfuls of baby spinach leaves, shredded
- 3 cloves of garlic, minced
- 2 tablespoons of extra-virgin olive oil
- 1 teaspoon of chili powder
- 1 tablespoon of cumin
- sea salt to taste
- pepper to taste
- fresh cilantro for garnish

**Directions:**

- Preheat oven to 350°F. Lightly grease a baking dish (approx. 9x13 inch) and set aside.
- In a large skillet, heat the prepared olive oil over medium heat. Sauté the onions for a few minutes, until they are translucent and lightly golden. Stir in garlic and sauté until fragrant. Pour in the tomato sauce and add the chili powder, cumin pepper and salt. Stir well and simmer for about 10 minutes.
- In a large bowl, combine the uncooked brown rice, broth, beans, tomato mixture and spinach. Stir well and transfer to the baking dish and top with the corn. Cover the baking dish with tin foil and bake for about 2 hours.
- When the rice is tender, remove from the oven, top with prepared fresh cilantro and serve warm.

# 38. Rice and Beans Colorful Dish

**Serving Size: 8**

**Preparation Time: 7 minutes**

**Cooking Time: 43 minutes**

**Ingredients:**

- ½ cup of rice
- ½ cup of raisings
- 1 medium red onion, diced
- 1 large carrot, grated
- 1 medium red bell pepper, diced
- 1 ½ cups of canned black beans, rinsed and drained
- 1 cup of snow peas
- 1 teaspoon of raw sugar
- 2 tablespoons of lime juice
- ½ teaspoon of salt
- 2 tablespoons of olive oil
- 1 teaspoon of dried ginger
- 2 tablespoons of chopped cilantro

**Directions:**

- In a large-sized bowl, whisk together lime juice, salt and sugar until dissolved. Set aside.
- Prepare the rice according to the package Directions.
- Meanwhile, in a wide skillet, heat the oil, add the onion, carrot and red pepper and sauté for 5 minutes, until tender. Stir in the ginger and peas and cook until the peas turn bright green, stirring frequently. Add the black beans, stir well and remove from the heat.
- When the rice is done, stir in the raisins and transfer the mixture into the skillet. Stir well to combine the rice and vegetables. Drizzle with lime juice and stir well again.
- Serve immediately with some chopped cilantro.

# 39. Rice and Chili Bean Pot

**Serving Size: 6**

**Preparation Time: 7 minutes**

**Cooking Time: 43 minutes**

**Ingredients:**

- 1 ¾ cups of canned kidney beans, drained and rinsed
- 3 cups of canned diced tomatoes
- 1 cup of wild rice
- 1 large brown onion, finely chopped
- 1 green capsicum, chopped
- 2 cloves of garlic, crushed
- 2 sticks of celery, sliced
- ¾ cups of thickly sliced mushrooms
- ½ cup of water
- 4 tablespoons of chili con carne mix
- 2 teaspoons of olive oil
- 2 tablespoons of tomato paste

**Directions:**

- Prepare the rice according to the package directions.
- In a large saucepan, heat the prepared oil over medium heat.
- Add the garlic and onion and cook for approximately about 5 minutes, until tender. Stir in the capsicum, tomato paste, chili con carne mix, mushrooms, and pour in the water. Cook, stirring occasionally, for 5 minutes.
- Add the prepared tomatoes and kidney beans and bring to a very hot boil. Reduce the heat to a heat of medium-low and simmer for about 35 minutes until the mixture thickens. Season with salt and pepper and serve warm.
- To serve, spoon the wild rice into the bowls and top with the bean mixture.

## 40. Rice, Bean, and Sausage Meal

**Serving Size: 8**

**Preparation Time: 20 minutes**

**Cooking Time: 40 minutes**

**Ingredients:**

- 1 cup of basmati rice
- salt and black pepper, to taste
- 1 tablespoon of vegetable oil
- 1 medium sweet onion, diced
- 1 green bell pepper, cored and diced
- 2 stalks of celery, diced
- 3 cloves of garlic, minced
- 2 tablespoons of tomato paste
- 1 ½ teaspoons of no-salt-added Cajun seasoning
- 1 teaspoon of hot sauce
- 1 (12.8-ounce) package of smoked Andouille sausage, thinly
- 3 cups of low-sodium chicken stock
- 1 bay leaf
- 3 (15-ounce) cans of red beans, drained and rinsed; or 15 ounces dry red beans, soaked and cooked
- 2 tablespoons of flat-leaf parsley, chopped

**Directions:**

- In a large saucepan, cook the prepared rice with 2 cups of water over medium-high heat following the package's instructions.
- Once the rice is cooked through, drain, and set aside.
- In a large stockpot/Dutch oven, heat oil over medium heat.
- Add the sausage and cook for 3-4 minutes or until evenly browned. Set aside to drain on a prepared plate lined with a paper towel.
- Add the bell pepper, onion, and celery. Cook until tender, about 3-4 minutes.
- Add the garlic, tomato paste, and Cajun seasoning. Cook for 1 minute or until fragrant.

- Add the hot sauce, stock, bay leaf, beans, and sausage. Season with freshly ground black pepper and salt to taste.
- Bring to a boil.
- Over low heat, cover, and simmer for about 15 minutes.
- Remove the cover and simmer until the mixture thickens, about another 15 minutes.
- Mash the beans slightly if you want to and then season with freshly ground black pepper and kosher salt to taste. Top with the parsley.
- Serve warm with the cooked rice.

# 41. Senegalese Rice and Beans with Yam

**Serving Size:** 8

**Preparation Time:** 7 minutes

**Cooking Time:** 22 minutes

**Ingredients:**

- 1 cup of black-eyed peas, pre-soaked
- 2 ½ cups of rice
- 2 ½ large onions, chopped
- 2 carrots, chopped
- 5 cloves of garlic, chopped
- 1 yam, chopped
- 1 vegetable bouillon cube
- ¾ cup of tomato paste
- ¼ cup of coconut oil
- 2 ½ teaspoons of salt
- ¼ teaspoon of hot pepper
- pepper to taste

**Directions:**

- Heat the prepared oil in a big pot over medium-high heat. Add the chopped onions and garlic and sauté until translucent. Pour in the tomato paste and stir well to combine the ingredients.
- Pour in about 5 cups of water and bring to the very hot boil. Add the beans, yams, carrots, vegetable bouillon cube, hot pepper, salt and pepper. Cook until the beans become tender.
- Stir in the rice, cover the pot and cook for 10 minutes. Uncover the pot and cook for another 10 minutes. Do not stir. If it appears to be to dry, pour in some more water. If it is too watery, cover the pot and cook covered for some time.
- Serve warm.

# 42. Shrimp White Bean Salad

**Serving Size: 4**

**Preparation Time: 10 minutes**

**Cooking Time: 4 minutes**

**Ingredients:**

- 8 cups of water
- 1 cup of dry white wine
- 1 pound of medium shrimp, shells on
- 1 ½ teaspoons of fresh rosemary, chopped
- 1 ½ teaspoons of lemon zest
- 3 tablespoons of lemon juice
- 1 ½ teaspoons of Dijon mustard
- ½ teaspoon of crushed red pepper flakes
- ¼ cup of extra-virgin olive oil
- 1 cup of dry cannellini beans, soaked and cooked
- 2 cups of cherry tomatoes, halved
- ⅔ cup of red onion, very thinly sliced
- 4 cups (about 5 ounces) packed baby arugula

**Directions:**

- In a large saucepan, boil the wine and water. Add the prepared shrimp and cook until opaque, about 4 minutes.
- Drain and rinse the shrimp under cold water, then dry.
- Peel the shrimp and remove the shells.
- In a medium-large salad bowl, add the chopped rosemary, lemon zest, lemon juice, mustard, and crushed red pepper flakes. Mix until well-combined.
- Drizzle the olive oil and whisk until well-combined.
- Add the beans, tomatoes, shrimp, and onion. Toss until well-combined.
- Add the arugula and toss again. Serve fresh.

# 43. South-African Fruity Beans and Rice

**Serving Size: 6**

**Preparation Time: 6 minutes**

**Cooking Time: 20 minutes**

**Ingredients:**

- ½ cup of rice
- 3 cups of canned kidney beans, drained
- 1 plump of vine tomatoes, coarsely chopped
- 1 ½ cup of boiling water
- 12 prunes, pitted
- 6 dried apricots
- ⅓ cup of sultanas or raisins
- 1 medium onions, finely chopped
- 1-2 green chilies, finely chopped
- 4 cloves of garlic, finely chopped
- 1 1-inch piece of ginger, peeled, finely chopped
- 1 small green pepper, coarsely chopped
- 1 cinnamon stick (approx. 3-inch piece)
- 1 ripe banana, thinly sliced
- ¼ cup of chopped toasted peanuts
- 2 tablespoons of sunflower oil
- 1 teaspoon of ground coriander
- 1 teaspoon of ground cumin
- 1 teaspoon of fennel seed
- lemon wedges

**Directions:**

- Bring a saucepan filled with water to the boil. Add the rice, reduce the heat and simmer until the rice is tender. When done, cover the pan and keep warm.
- In a small saucepan, add the boiling water along with the dried fruit. Cover the pan and bring to the boil. Reduce the heat and simmer for about 20 min. or until plump. Do not drain the fruit.

- In the meantime, heat a large saucepan and pour in the oil. Add the onions and fry until lightly golden. Stir in the chilies, garlic, green pepper, ginger and all the spices. Cook for about 1-2 minutes, stirring frequently.
- Add the kidney beans, chopped tomatoes and salt. Stir in the fruit together with the water. When it eventually starts boiling, reduce the heat and simmer for 30 minutes, stirring occasionally.
- Serve warm, on top of the cooked rice. Sprinkle with the toasted peanuts, lemon wedges and a few slices of banana.

# 44. Spicy Rice and Beans

**Serving Size: 6**

**Preparation Time: 6 minutes**

**Cooking Time: 22 minutes**

**Ingredients:**

- 1 ½ cups of canned pinto beans, drained
- 1 ½ cups of long-grain brown rice
- 2 ¾ cups of water
- ½ cup of grated carrot
- ½ cup of chopped celery
- 1 cup of chopped onion
- ½ cup of fresh corn (or ½ cup frozen corn)
- 1 cup of chopped tomato
- 3 cloves of garlic mixed
- 1 jalapeño pepper, seeded, finely diced
- 1 teaspoon of ground cumin
- 1 tablespoon of canola oil
- 2 teaspoons of chili powder
- 1 teaspoon of ground coriander
- 1 bay leaf
- 1 tablespoon of vegetable bouillon granules
- 2 tablespoons of fresh parsley
- 1 tablespoon of chopped fresh cilantro (optional)

**Directions:**

- Pour the canola oil into a large frying pan and heat it over medium heat. Add the garlic, onion, jalapeño pepper, and celery and sauté for 3 minutes, stirring occasionally. Stir in the chili powder, coriander, cumin, and rice.
- Cook on medium heat until golden, stirring occasionally.
- Add the carrot, bay leaf, and bouillon powder and pour in water. Cover the pan and simmer for about 20 minutes.

- Stir in the tomato, beans, and corn. Cover the pot again and simmer for 15-20 more minutes until the liquid has been absorbed.
- Once done, remove and discard the bay leaf. Add the chopped cilantro (optional) and 1 tbsp of parsley.
- Serve warm and finish with the remaining parsley.

# 45. Spicy Taco Beans and Rice

**Serving Size: 4**

**Preparation Time: 8 minutes**

**Cooking Time: 50 minutes**

**Ingredients:**

- 1 tablespoon of oil
- ½ cup of dehydrated chopped onion, reconstituted
- ¼ cup of dehydrated or freeze dried chopped green bell pepper, reconstituted
- 2 cans of pinto or black beans (or a mix), drained (or 3 cups cooked beans)
- 1 tablespoon of taco seasoning
- 1 teaspoon of dried parsley
- 1 (15 ounce) can diced tomatoes, undrained
- 3 cups of cooked rice

**Directions:**

- Heat oil in a medium-sized pan.
- Add onion and bell pepper and cook for 2-3 minutes or until tender.
- Add beans, taco seasoning, parsley, and tomatoes.
- Bring to a boil, then lower heat.
- Simmer for about 30 minutes, stirring often.
- Serve over cooked rice.

# 46. Spinach and White Bean Soup

**Serving Size: 4**

**Preparation Time: 8 minutes**

**Cooking Time: 40 minutes**

**Ingredients:**

- 2 tablespoons of dehydrated minced garlic
- ¼ cup of dehydrated chopped onion
- 1 teaspoon of dried basil
- 1 cup of freeze-dried chopped spinach
- 2 cans of white beans, undrained (or 3 cups cooked)
- 4-5 cups of chicken or vegetable broth

**Directions:**

- Add all ingredients to a medium stock pot.
- Bring to a very hot boil, then lower heat to medium.
- Simmer for 35 Minutes to 1 hour.

# 47. Spinach Lentil Pasta

**Serving Size: 4**

**Preparation Time: 7 minutes**

**Cooking Time: 55 minutes**

**Ingredients:**

- 1 can of green lentils, drained
- 1 can of tomato puree
- 4 cups of spinach, finely chopped
- 1 medium sized onion, minced
- 3 cloves of garlic, minced
- ½ package of jumbo pasta shells (about 20 pieces)
- 1 medium size carrot, diced
- 1 celery stalk, diced
- 3 tablespoons of olive oil
- 1 sprig of fresh thyme, chopped
- cayenne
- parmesan cheese

**Directions:**

- Cook pasta al dente according to packet directions.
- Sauté onion and garlic in olive oil. Add celery and thyme and cook until fragrant.
- Add carrot, tomato puree, and lentils, and bring to a simmer. Leave the heat on until the carrot is cooked.
- Add cayenne to taste.
- Pour sauce over pasta and finish with parmesan cheese before serving.

# 48. STUFFED ACORN SQUASH WITH BEANS AND RICE

**Serving Size: 4**

**Preparation Time: 4 minutes**

**Cooking Time: 21 minutes**

**Ingredients:**

- ½ cup of brown basmati rice
- 1 acorn squash, cleaned, halved
- 1 ½ cups of canned black beans, drained and rinsed
- 1 medium onion, chopped
- 2 cloves of garlic
- 1 cup of sliced carrots
- 1 red pepper, chopped
- ½ cup of chopped fresh cilantro
- 2 tablespoons of olive oil
- 2 tablespoons of agave nectar
- a handful of raisins
- ¼ - ½ teaspoon of turmeric
- salt to taste
- pepper to taste

**Directions:**

- Preheat the oven to 350°F.
- Prepare the rice, by cooking it in a saucepan filled with water. When it actually starts boiling, reduce the heat and simmer until tender.
- Drizzle the acorn squash halves with the agave nectar. Place them in a baking dish and roast for about 30 minutes until tender. Add a few tablespoons of water while roasting to retain moisture.
- Heat the olive oil in a large-sized skillet over medium-high meat. Add the carrots, onions, garlic, red pepper and raisins and fry until tender. Stir in the turmeric and cooked rice and mix well.
- Add the chopped cilantro and black beans and stir well to combine. Remove from the heat.

- When the squash is done, you can drizzle it again with agave nectar, if desired, and then stuff it with the beans and rice mixture.
- Return to the oven and cook for 10 more minutes if needed. Do not overcook it.
- When done, cut the halves so as to get 4 pieces total and serve.

# 49. Tofu and Rice and Lentils Curry

**Serving Size: 4**

**Preparation Time: 7 minutes**

**Cooking Time: 43 minutes**

**Ingredients:**

- ½ cup of spit red lentils
- 1 cup of chopped green beans, topped
- 10 ounces of firm tofu, chopped
- ⅓ cup of chopped fresh coriander
- 1 cup of basmati rice
- 1 medium brown onion, chopped
- 2 ½ cups of vegetable stock
- 11 ounces of cauliflower, cut into florets
- 2 medium carrots, peeled and sliced
- 10-inch piece of ginger, peeled and finely chopped
- 1 large fresh chili, halved, deseeded, chopped
- 2 teaspoons of garam masala
- 1 teaspoon of ground turmeric
- salt to taste
- pepper to taste

**Directions:**

- Bring to the boil a saucepan filled with water. Reduce the heat, add the rice and cook until tender.
- In a large saucepan, heat the prepared oil over medium heat. Add the onion and sauté for approximately about 5 minutes.
- When the onion is soft, add the ginger, garam masala and turmeric and cook for 1 minute, stirring.
- Pour in the prepared vegetable stock, add the cauliflower, lentils, chili and carrots.
- Bring to the very hot boil, reduce the heat to medium-low and simmer, covered for about 15 minutes.

- Add the beans and tofu and cook for 10 more minutes.
- When the vegetables are done, season with salt and pepper and gently stir the coriander.
- Serve immediately with hot rice.

# 50. Tuna Bean Casserole

**Serving Size: 4**

**Preparation Time: 8 minutes**

**Cooking Time: 55 minutes**

**Ingredients:**

- ¼ cup of sour cream powder
- 1 can of condensed cream of mushroom soup
- 1 (5 ounce) can of tuna, drained
- 2 (15 ounce) cans of pinto or black beans, drained
- ½ teaspoon of garlic salt
- ¼ teaspoon of ground black pepper
- ¼ cup of dehydrated chopped onion, reconstituted
- 2 cups of cooked pasta of choice
- 1 cup of freeze-dried grated cheddar cheese, reconstituted

**Directions:**

- Preheat oven to 350°F.
- Cook pasta according to package directions. Reconstitute onion and cheese in separate bowls.
- In a large-sized bowl, combine all ingredients except cheese. Pour mixture into greased 13 x 9 baking dish. Sprinkle cheese over top. Bake uncovered for 45 minutes or until golden brown and bubbly.

# 51. Turkey Bean One-Pot Rice

**Serving Size: 8**

**Preparation Time: 10 minutes**

**Cooking Time: 55 minutes**

**Ingredients:**

- 1 tablespoon of olive oil
- 2 pounds of ground turkey
- 1 ½ teaspoons of ground cumin
- 1 ½ teaspoons of dried oregano
- 1 ½ teaspoons of onion powder
- 1 ½ teaspoons of garlic powder
- ½ teaspoon of freshly ground black pepper
- 1 teaspoon of kosher salt
- 2 red bell peppers, cored and diced
- 2 tablespoons of tomato paste
- 1 tablespoon of apple cider vinegar
- 2 (15.5-ounce) cans of red kidney beans, drained and rinsed; or 10 ounces of dry red kidney beans, soaked and cooked
- 2 cups of low-sodium chicken broth
- 1 cup of jasmine rice

**Directions:**

- Season the turkey with ground cumin, dried oregano, onion powder, garlic powder, freshly ground black pepper, and kosher salt. Set aside for 15 minutes to marinate.
- In a medium saucepan or skillet, heat oil over medium heat.
- Add the turkey and cook until evenly browned about 5-6 minutes.
- Add the bell peppers and cook for 2 minutes.
- Create a pocket in the center of the mixture, then pour the vinegar and tomato paste into the pocket.
- Stir gently and cook for 30 seconds.
- Add in the beans, rice, and broth.

- Stir until everything is well-combined.
- Bring to a boil.
- Over low heat, cover and simmer for about 40-45 minutes or until rice is tender.
- Serve whilst warm.

# 52. White Beans and Corn Chili

**Serving Size: 14**

**Preparation Time: 10 minutes**

**Cooking Time: 45 minutes**

**Ingredients:**

- 1 pound of white beans, which are soaked for 6 hours and then washed in 6 cups of chicken broth
- 1 pound of frozen corn
- 1 medium onion, chopped
- 7 ounces of green chilies in a canister
- 6 cloves of garlic
- 4 teaspoons of ground cumin
- 1 teaspoon of dried oregano
- 2 teaspoons of cayenne pepper

**Directions:**

- Add enough water to create the Dutch on high heat to boil beans. Cook until the beans are soft.
- Then, lower the heat to an actual simmer and cook for about 30 minutes.
- Clean the beans thoroughly, then put them in the bowl.
- Divide beans among seven (1-pint) sterilized containers.
- Each jar must be filled with hot broth mix.
- Use a knife to cut through the Jars to eliminate air bubbles.
- Use a damp kitchen towel to clean any food remnants off the rims of the bottles.
- The lid must seal each jar.
- Place the jars in the pressurized canner. A process with 10 pounds of pressure for 75 minutes.
- Set the jars on a wooden surface about a foot from each other to allow them to cool.
- Once the jars are cooled, you can use your fingers to press each container's lids until the seal has been sealed.
- The canning jars must be kept in cool and dark areas.

# 53. White Bean and Vegetable Ragout

**Serving Size: 4**

**Preparation Time: 7 minutes**

**Cooking Time: 55 minutes**

**Ingredients:**

- 1 cup of frozen dried sliced carrots, reconstituted
- 1/2 cup of freeze-dried zucchini, reconstituted
- 1 (15 ounce) can of diced tomatoes, drained
- ¼ cup of freeze dried diced red or green bell peppers, reconstituted
- 2 (15 ounce) cans of white beans, drained
- 2 teaspoons of dry minced garlic
- 4 cups of chicken broth
- tomato paste
- ¼ teaspoon of salt, more to taste
- ground black pepper to taste

**Directions:**

- Reconstitute carrots, zucchini, and bell peppers in same bowl.
- Combine all ingredients in a medium stock pot.
- Bring to a boil.
- Lower heat and simmer for 30 minutes to 1 hour.

# 54. White Bean Chili Wraps

**Serving Size: 4**

**Preparation Time: 10 minutes**

**Cooking Time: 5 minutes**

**Ingredients:**

- 2 teaspoons of canned and finely chopped chipotles in adobo sauce
- 2 tablespoons of apple cider vinegar
- 1 tablespoon of canola oil
- ¼ teaspoon of kosher salt
- ¼ cup of cilantro, chopped
- 2 cups of red cabbage, shredded
- 1 medium carrot, peeled and shredded
- 1 can of white beans, rinsed; or 5 ounces dry white beans, soaked and cooked
- 1 ripe avocado, pitted and chopped
- ½ cup of sharp cheddar cheese, shredded
- 2 tablespoons of red onion, minced
- 4 (8-10 inch) tortillas or whole-wheat wraps

**Directions:**

- In a large mixing bowl, add the chipotle, vinegar, oil, and kosher salt. Mix until well-combined.
- Add the cilantro, cabbage, and carrot. Toss to mix well.
- In another bowl, add the avocado and beans. Mash until smooth, then add the onion and cheese. Mix until well-combined.
- To make the wraps, add ½ cup of the bean mixture in the center of each tortilla.
- Add ⅔ cup cabbage slaw to each tortilla, then roll the tortillas to seal the wraps.
- Serve fresh.

# 55. White Beans

**Serving Size: 28**

**Preparation Time: 8 minutes**

**Cooking Time: 35 minutes**

**Ingredients:**

- 3 ¼ pounds of dried white beans, soaked for 18 hours and drained
- 4 ½ teaspoons of salt

**Directions:**

- In a Dutch oven, add beans and enough water to cover over high heat and cook until boiling. Adjust the heat to low then cook for about 30 minutes.
- Drain the beans, reserving cooking liquid. In 7 (1-pint) hot sterilized jars, divide the beans and sprinkle with salt.
- Fill each jar with hot cooking liquid, leaving 1-inch space from the top. Run your knife around the insides of each jar to remove any air bubbles.
- Clean any trace of food off the rims of jars with a clean, moist kitchen towel. Close each jar with a lid and screw on the ring.
- Carefully place the jars in the pressure canner and eventually process at 10 pounds pressure for about 75 minutes.
- Remove the jars from pressure canner and place onto a wood surface several inches apart to cool completely.
- After cooling with your finger, press the top of each jar's lid to ensure that the seal is tight. Store these canning jars in a cool, dark place.

# Chapter 7.
# Other Tips to Store Food for Survival Use

Being a successful prepper requires proper storage and you should prepare a storage room to handle your storage needs. You have to focus on light, pests, moisture, time and temperature because the food can be spoiled due to humidity and excessive sunlight. You can build a wooden shed or a temporary room to store your preserved food items. It will be good to install shelves in your room to get extra storage space. There are a few tips to preserve food items:

## Drying

Drying is a great way to preserve fruits, herbs, vegetables, and meats. If you want to dry herbs, you can tie them together and hang in a sunny place. You have to dry moisture out of food to protect it for a longer period of time. This practice is used throughout the world, such as southern Italy, where it is famous to dry tomatoes and India which is famous for drying mangoes and chilies. If you want to dry herbs, you can hang them in a sunny place away from moisture. You can dry fruits and vegetables by placing them on a clean surface, but select a sunny place to keep them in the sun for a few weeks. This method works the best in warm and dry climates. The electric dehydrating machine is a modern method to dry fruits and vegetables.

## Salting

Salting is a small category of the drying method. You can add salt to foods, such as fish and meat to extract moisture. This will reduce the bacterial content and make the food flexible for later use. Salt can make animal protein a bit leathery. Beef jerky and salted cod are famous food items prepared with preserved meat.

## Canning

If you want to can food, you have to heat the food. This technique was developed by a French chemist in 1790, his name was Nicolas Appert. This method was used to preserve food for Napoleon's army. It is a popular way to preserve fruits, meats, and vegetables. You can use both cans and glass jars to preserve food. It is important to sterilize these cans in boiling water along with lids for a few minutes. You can fill these cans and glass jars with jam, jelly or other content. Add brine or sugar syrup in the cans. After filling, you should secure the lid firmly, but don't make it too tight.

It is then time to place the jars in a pot with water, cover it and let it boil. You have to process if for almost ten minutes at a full boil and then pull the jars or cans out from the hot water and let it cool. They will seal like a vacuum as they cooled down. Cooking time will actually vary depending on what you're canning.

## Freezing

Now, you have electrical freezers to preserve your foods. These freezers can change the texture of the most vegetables and fruits, but the fish and meat will not change their texture. In the summer, you can freeze your berries to make smoothies and bake cakes. It will be good to freeze fruits and vegetables in batches. For instance, you can spread out fresh berries or other fruits on a baking tray and place it in the freezer. Once they become solid, you can put them in a bag.

You should freeze fresh food as quickly as possible to keep it at zero degrees. Packaging food in the freezer containers will avoid any deterioration. There is no need to open container in the freezer because the dry air of the freezer will deteriorate the food. There are a few things to avoid freezer burn:

Reduce Exposure to Air: You should wrap the food tightly to avoid exposure to dry air.

Avoid Fluctuating Temperature: It is essential to keep freezer closed as much as you can, and try to determine the name of things that you want to remove from freezer, before opening it.

Don't Overfill Freezer: Use caution to not over-fill the freezer because it will reduce the circulation of air and increase the speed of the damage.

### Fermentation

Fermenting is fairly similar to canning, although you don't have to seal up the food and allow the entry of good bacteria. You can use acidic brine because brine helps you to control the fermentation of your food by selecting anaerobic bacteria, kill potentially harmful molds and bacteria strains to conserve your produce against breakdown.

### Salt Curing and Brining

It is an old method to preserve meat because the salt creates an inhospitable environment for bacteria and microorganism. You can rub the mixture of sugar and salt on the pieces of fresh meat, pack it tightly into a crock and store it in a stable place and cool temperature. Salt-curing requires you to soak meat in water for a long time to remove the excess salt and bring it to an edible level.

# CONCLUSION

Everyone who is old enough to remember 2020 has experienced a small sample of what can happen when things get bad. You can't prepare for everything. You can't have every possible contingency for every imaginable disaster. The goal isn't to be perfect.

A nutritionist friend once gave me a little piece of advice. I asked her if she had any good rules of thumb for eating well. She answered, "When you are in the grocery store, look ahead of you and behind you. What are the other people in line ahead and behind you eating? Are you eating healthier than they are?"

If you are eating healthier than the two people standing near you, you are 67th percentile of nutritious eating. If you go to the grocery store again, and you are still eating better than they are, you're in the 75th percentile. A third time, you're in the 85th percentile, etc. I don't need to be the most prepared person imaginable. With a little bit of preparation, I am already more prepared to protect my family and my property than are 99% of people.

If you have a tool for hunting or trapping, camping equipment, means to collect water and clean it, basic emergency medical supplies, and a few pounds of rice and beans, you are already in better shape than almost everyone in the town you live in.

Humans have survived some of the most horrific conditions imaginable. We are all the descendants of these people. We are all the descendants of an unbroken chain of survivors that traces all the way back to the beginning of life on this planet. Every person has the potential to continue in that tradition.

It doesn't take much to prep. It doesn't require a major lifestyle choice or a set of beliefs or politics. All it requires is a little bit of knowledge and a little bit of effort and mindfulness to become a person who can get themselves - and the people they love - through things that countless humans went through long before us.

# PREPPER'S WATER SURVIVAL GUIDE

THE DISASTER-PROOF LOW BUDGET WAY
TO FIND, HARVEST, PURIFY, STORE ENDLESS WATER.
BUILD A SUSTAINABLE FILTRATION SYSTEM,
BE SELF-SUFFICIENT
AND THRIVE OFF THE GRID

Reed Parker

# TABLE OF CONTENTS

# INTRODUCTION

Water is one of the essentials of human life, and it is one that many people take for granted. Many people fail to drink enough water when it is readily available, resulting in different symptoms. However, when one is lost in the wilderness, not drinking water can result in your death within three days.

Even if you go on a planned hike, there is always a chance that you get turned around and can't find your way back. Although you may have packed enough water for your planned hike, likely, it will not last long.

If you have planned your hike perfectly, you will know where the large catchments of water are (lakes, rivers, etc.). However, you should never drink directly from these sources, as you do not know what microorganisms or pollution may be present.

Only collect water from fast-flowing water sources found at a higher elevation to avoid some dangers. It is vital to read your environment. If no plants grow around a water source, or if you note many animal bones, this could indicate pollution.

Also, note if there are any mineral deposits around the water's edge. This may indicate highly alkaline-content water, which you shouldn't drink from.

Be observant. Plants and animals will also give you clues as to where you can find water. Many herbivorous animals travel along well-established game trails to get to a water supply, and you can follow fresh tracks to find their water source. They are an indicator of there still being water. You can dig a hole at the base of their roots then wait until the liquid starts to pool before you collect it.

# CHAPTER I.
# WHAT IS PREPPING?

You may be asking yourself, "What are we prepping for?" It can be anything from natural disasters to societal collapse, and it's important to be prepared no matter what. There are times when being prepared will save your life. Whether you live in a small town or a large city, being prepared is the only way to protect your family and your home.

The first step in prepping is to consider the food and water requirements of your family. The most important resource in an emergency is water, which we depend on for hygiene and sanitation. Then, you need to stock up on non-perishable food items. Ideally, you'll need about 30 days' worth of food. Buying extra food every time you go grocery shopping will be crucial to maintaining your food supply.

It's important to remember that the cold war was only a few decades ago, but there was a very real risk of nuclear war. In the coming decades, tensions with China and North Korea may escalate to the point where a nuclear war may break out. In addition, Russia and Iran may have nuclear weapons. In addition, terrorist attacks can be a very real threat.

Survivalism, also known as prepping, is a social movement that prepares for emergencies. Preppers aim to be self-sufficient, well protected from disasters, and able to survive until the coast is clear. While most preppers plan for natural disasters, others prepare for catastrophic events.

A bug-out bag is an essential prepping item. This bag allows the prepper to quickly escape the home in an emergency. It should be filled with food, water, and first aid gear. It should be kept in a convenient location near the door. Prepping should also include ways to stay clean and sanitary. It is also important to outfit your vehicle with protection in case you must evacuate.

Some studies have found a connection between prepping and anxiety. Preppers often express concerns about the availability of resources and the safety of other people. This may be a result of their pessimistic outlook. They are also fixated on negative events in the future. This can lead to an anxiety-producing situation.

Prepping behaviors and beliefs are influenced by our daily experiences. When we are exposed to stressors such as an epidemic, we tend to interpret it as a doomsday scenario. Consequently, our beliefs and behaviors are often negatively influenced by these experiences. The stress associated with these experiences may be contributing factors to our prepping behaviors.

Preparing for an earthquake can also help us cope with disasters that may strike. We need to be aware that these things can strike anytime. If we are not ready for them, we will not be able to respond appropriately.

# Developing a Positive Attitude of Survival

Developing a positive mental attitude is an integral part of survival. It allows you to make better decisions and combat unconscious stress. It also allows you to be more alert and aware of your surroundings. It can help you resist unwanted neighbors or respond to threats without fear. It's a very important skill to cultivate even before SHTF.

Your survival will depend on your attitude and your ability to adapt to any situation. It will require creativity, innovation, and self-reliance. You must be able to work with nature, improvise, and solve problems to survive. You must be able to use your resources to your advantage. The key is to use the environment to your advantage and make the most of your skills and resources.

Developing a positive attitude is a good first step toward surviving a survival situation. It will help you make the best decisions possible, so you should practice it often. For example, try to imitate the steps a cat takes to go from the inside to the outside. You should also practice taking deep breaths and relaxing. Having a positive attitude will also help you trust your own intuition more.

It is important to learn about your personality and the way it affects your survival. If you have a negative attitude, you are less likely to make the best decisions, and your chances of survival will be lower. People who have a positive attitude will be more positive, and will react to a difficult situation with more positivity and optimism. Developing a positive outlook will make the difference between survival and death.

There are several studies that have explored the importance of psychological attributes in disaster response. In a recent study, researchers have found that the psychological attributes associated with an increased probability of survival were linked to a range of behaviors. The study used existing literature on the psychology of survival to develop a fifteen-item self-report questionnaire to measure a person's attitude towards survival. The questionnaire yields three dimensions of the survival attitude: resilience, optimism, and social desirability.

Fear, hope, and genetics are factors that affect our survival. When a person is afraid of an impending situation, they must learn to cope with the negative emotions and negative experiences. They should be grateful for any silver linings and look for the positives that exist in the situation. This will transform the person's entire outlook. The ability to face and overcome negative feelings will help them survive in any situation. A positive attitude can also be a good mental attitude.

If you are confronted with an emergency situation, you must have the right mindset to make the right decisions. A negative mental attitude will hinder your ability to reason and solve problems. If you think that you can't survive, you will not try to survive. You must have a clear goal for your life. A positive mindset will help you adapt to the situation and help you avoid becoming hopeless in the face of loneliness.

# Chapter 2.
# Understand the Situation and Understand Preparedness

So here we are, in the actual midst of a global pandemic. As a prepper, one of the most important things you can do is to have a plan for finding water. Whether you're bugging out in the wilderness or hunkering down at home, access to clean water is essential for survival. Here are some tips for finding water that you can rely on in an emergency:

One of the best ways to find water is to look for natural sources like rivers, lakes, and ponds. If you're bugging out in the wilderness, these can be lifesavers. However, it's important to remember that any water you find in the wild will need to be treated before you drink it. Boiling is the best way to kill bacteria and make water safe to drink.

Another option is to collect rainwater. This can be done by using a tarp or other impermeable material to catch rainfall. Once you've collected the rainwater, it will need to be filtered before you drink it. One easy way to do this is by using a coffee filter.

Finally, if you're hunkering down at home during an emergency, your best bet is to stock up on bottled water ahead of time. This will ensure that you have enough clean water to last until the crisis has passed.

One of the most important things to consider when collecting water is the quality of the source. If you are using a groundwater source, be sure to test it for contaminants before use. Surface water sources, such as rivers and lakes, should also be tested before use. Once you have determined that your water source is safe, you can begin collecting water.

In an emergency, every drop of water counts. That's why it's important to have a few water collectors on hand in case your tap water is cut off or contaminated. Water collectors come in all shapes and sizes, from small emergency containers to large barrels. They can be made of plastic, metal, or even glass. No matter what material you choose, make sure that your water collector is food-grade and BPA-free. This will ensure that the water inside is safe to drink. If you live in an area prone to hurricanes or other natural disasters, it's also a good idea to have a water collector in your basement or garage. That way, you'll have access to clean drinking water even if your power goes out.

There are a few more different methods that can be used to collect water, including hand pumps, buckets, and troughs. Each method has its own advantages and disadvantages, so it is important to choose the right one for your needs. Hand pumps are typically used for small-scale water collection, while buckets and troughs are better suited for larger volumes of water.

Once you have collected your water, it is important to store it in a clean, safe container. Be sure to label your containers so that you know which water is safe to drink and which should be used for other purposes, such as washing or cooking. Water that has been treated with chemicals, such as chlorine, should be clearly labeled and stored away from other sources of drinking water.

With these tips, you can be sure that you'll always have access to clean water in an emergency situation.

# HOW TO COLLECT RAINWATER

One of the best ways to collect rainwater is with a rain barrel. A rain barrel is a container that you can place under your downspout to collect water as it runs off your roof.

Another way to collect rainwater is with a cistern. A cistern is a larger container that can be used to store more water. Cisterns are typically buried underground and can be used for irrigation or other purposes.

If you live in an area with frequent rainfall, you may want to consider installing a rainwater harvesting system. This type of system captures rainwater from your roof and stores it in a tank for later use.

Here are some tips on how to harvest rainwater from your roof:

- Install a rain barrel or catchment system at the base of your downspouts.
- Make sure that your barrels or tanks are covered to keep out debris and Mosquitoes.
- Direct the overflow from your barrels or tanks away from your foundation.
- By following these simple tips, you can easily harvest rainwater from your roof.

If you're interested in collecting rainwater, there are a few things you need to keep in mind. First, make sure you have the right equipment. Second, be sure to collect the water from a clean area so that it's safe to use. And finally, be sure to properly clean and maintain your rain barrel or cistern so that it will last for years to come. With a little bit of planning and effort, collecting rainwater can be a great way to save water.

Is rainwater harvesting worth it?

Although rainwater harvesting systems can be expensive to install, they offer a number of advantages. Rainwater is free, and it can be used for a variety of purposes, including watering plants and cleaning. In addition, rainwater harvesting can help to reduce flooding by redirecting water away from storm drains and into storage tanks. And perhaps most importantly, rainwater harvesting helps to conserve water, which is an increasingly scarce resource. For all of these reasons, rainwater harvesting is definitely worth considering.

# How to reliably find water in a desert

Water is not always easy to find, especially in the desert. Although it may seem like there is no water in the desert, there actually is water. It just takes a little bit of effort to find it. There are several ways to find water in the desert, including looking for signs of life, searching for water sources, and collecting morning dew. With a little bit of knowledge and effort, anyone can find water in the desert and survive.

In the desert, water is a precious commodity. Without it, survival is impossible. But where does water come from in such a dry place? It turns out that there is water all around us in the desert, even if we can't see it. Plants and animals release water vapor into the air through a process called evaporation.

For the prepper, being able to find water in a desert is a vital skill. With temperatures often reaching over 100 degrees Fahrenheit, dehydration is a real danger. And without water, survival is simply not possible. So how can you find water in a desert?

One of the most obvious places to look for water is cacti. Although they may seem dry and lifeless, cacti actually store water in their leaves and stems. Cacti are a great source of water in a desert environment. Although they may not look like it, cacti are actually quite adept at storing water. In fact, some cacti can store up to 30 gallons of water in their fleshy stems. To find water in a cactus, start by looking for ones that are green and healthy-looking. These are more likely to have plenty of water inside them. Once you've found a suitable cactus, cut it open with a knife and scoop out the water with a container. The water inside a cactus isn't always the best-tasting, but in a survival situation, it's better than nothing.

Another good place to look for water is near cliffs or rocky outcroppings. These areas are often cooler than the surrounding desert and can be home to springs or seeps. While these areas might not have any water at the surface, there is often water seeping through the rocks.

Finally, don't forget about animal trails. Animals know where the water is, so following their tracks can lead you to a hidden oasis. Animals have a keen sense of smell and can often sniff out water sources that are hidden from human view. In addition, they often know where to find the best sources of water, meaning that following them can lead you to pockets of water that you would otherwise never find. Of course, this isn't always an easy task. Animals can be elusive and hard to track, and the hot desert sun can quickly take its toll on even the most experienced tracker. But if you're lost in the desert and desperate for water, following the animals is one of the best chances you have for finding your way to safety.

Also, insects need water to survive, so they will often be attracted to sources of water. By following a trail of flying insects, you can often find a water source. If there are no flying insects around, you can also look for other signs of water, such as green plants or damp sand. With a little effort, you should be able to find the water you need to survive in the desert.

Another way to find water is to follow lizards and snakes. These animals are good at finding sources of water, and they will often lead you to a watering hole or other source of fresh water. Of course, it is important to be careful when following these creatures, as some species of lizard and snake can be poisonous. However, if you exercise caution and common sense, you can rely on these helpful animals to lead you to the precious resource of water in the desert.

You can also look for birds. Birds need water to drink and bathe, so they are always on the lookout for sources of water. They will often perch on high ground so that they can see a large area, and they will fly back and forth to different sources of water. By watching birds, it is possible to get a good sense of where the best sources of water are. Just be sure to follow the bird's lead, as they will usually know where the safest and most reliable sources of water can be found. With these tips in mind, you should be able to find water even in the most hostile desert conditions.

## HOW TO RELIABLY FIND WATER IN A COLD ENVIRONMENT

In the winter, water becomes a vital resource. With survival being the key, it is essential to know how to find water in a cold environment. Although water can be found in many forms, the purest and most reliable source is ice. To find ice, look for snowbanks or areas where the sun does not hit as often. These are generally the places where ice will form first. Chipping away at the ice will give you access to pure water that you can then boil or filter for further safety. Knowing how to find water in a cold environment is a critical survival skill.

Once you find the snow or ice, remember: Don't eat it!

Indeed, one of the most important things to remember is: don't eat the snow. That may sound like a strange warning, but there's a good reason for it. Eating snow can lower your body temperature, which can lead to hypothermia. In addition, snow can contain harmful bacteria that can make you sick. So, if you're stranded in a winter storm, resist the temptation to nibble on the snow. Stick to melting it for drinking water instead. By following this simple rule, you'll increase your chances of making it through the winter safe and sound.

In a winter wilderness, water is one of the most important things to find. Without it, you will quickly become dehydrated and your body will not be able to function properly. Here are some of the best places to look for water in a winter wilderness:

- **Melting ice** :Ice is a great source of water, but you need to be careful that you do not drink water that has been contaminated by melted snow. If you can find a clean source of ice, then it can be a great way to stay hydrated.

- **Rivers and Streams**: These are another great source of water, but you need to be careful of the water level as it can change quickly in a winter environment. Make sure you purify any water you take from these sources.

- **Ponds and Lakes**: These can also be a great source of water, but you need to be careful as they can freeze over quickly in winter. Again, make sure you purify any water you take from these sources.

- **Plants**: Plants can also provide a source of water, but you need to be careful as some plants contain toxins that could make you sick. Only drink from plants that you know are safe.

Survival in a winter wilderness depends on being able to find sources of water. By knowing where to look, you can increase your chances of finding the water you need to stay alive.

# How to reliably find water using municipal water supplies

With survival being one of the most important things to think about when preparing for an emergency is how you will find water. While it's true that there are many ways to collect and purify water in the wilderness, it's also true that these methods can be time-consuming and unreliable. A much smarter strategy is to take advantage of municipal water supplies. With a little planning, you can easily tap into these sources of potable water, even in the event of a power outage. One of the most reliable methods is to fill large containers with water before the emergency strikes. This way, you'll have a ready supply of clean water on hand without having to worry about purification. Another useful method is to invest in a gravity-fed water filtration system. These systems rely on gravity to force water through a series of filters, leaving you with clean, potable water. In addition, many municipal water supplies now contain fluoride, which can help to prevent tooth decay. By taking advantage of these resources, you can be sure that you and your family will always have access to clean drinking water.

Every day, we rely on municipal water supplies for drinking, cooking, and cleaning. We trust that the government agencies responsible for ensuring the quality of our water are working to protect us from harmful toxins. However, occasionally toxins do slip through the cracks and end up in our water. When this happens, it's important to take steps to protect yourself and your family. First, find out if your water supply has been affected. This information should be available from your local government or water utility. If there is a problem, avoid using tap water for drinking, cooking, or brushing your teeth. Stick to bottled water or water that has been boiled for at least three minutes. You should also take care to disinfect any surfaces that have come into contact with contaminated water. Regularly cleaning and disinfecting these areas will help to prevent the spread of toxins. By taking these precautions, you can protect yourself and your family from harm.

What should you do if municipal water is contaminated?

One of the most important things you can do to protect your health is to ensure that the water you drink is safe. Unfortunately, water contamination is a widespread problem, and even municipal water supplies can be contaminated with harmful microbes or chemicals. If you suspect that your water may not be safe to drink, there are a few steps you can take to protect yourself. First, try to find out if there have been any recent reports of water contamination in your area. You can also have your water tested for contaminants at a local lab. If you decide not to drink the water, you can purify it using a home filtration system or by boiling it for at least three minutes.

# How to Reliably Find Water Using a Dug Well

There are many different types of wells that can be used to access water, and each has its own advantages and disadvantages.

One of the most common types of wells is a dug well. These wells are relatively easy and inexpensive to construct, and they can be a good option for those who are planning to use their water supply for general household purposes. However, dug wells can be susceptible to contamination, so they may not be the best choice for those who are looking to survive in an emergency situation.

Another type of well is a drilled well. These wells require more resources and expertise to construct, but they can provide a cleaner water source that is less likely to be contaminated. This makes them a good option for preppers who want to have a reliable water supply in case of an emergency.

Finally, there are also drilled water wells. These wells are the deepest and most expensive to construct, but they can provide an incredibly reliable water source. They may not be feasible for everyone, but they can be a good option for those who want to be sure that they have access to clean water in an emergency situation.

When it comes to digging a well, start by finding an area where there is likely to be underground water, such as near a river or stream. Then, use a shovel to dig a hole that is at least six feet deep. Once the hole is dug, place a bucket in the hole and use a rope to lower it down. When the bucket reaches the bottom of the hole, start pulling it up slowly. As the bucket fills with water, it will become heavier, so be careful not to over-exert yourself. Once the bucket is full, remove it from the hole and place it in a safe location. Repeat this process until you have collected enough water for your needs. With a little effort, you can easily find water using a dug well.

However, there are many things to consider before drilling your own well. While it may seem like a good idea to save money and have more control over your water supply, there are a number of potential risks involved. First of all, drilling can be a dangerous process. If you don't have the proper training or equipment, you could seriously injure yourself or even cause death. In addition, there is always the possibility that you could contaminate your water supply with bacteria or chemicals.

Even if you take all the necessary precautions, there's no guarantee that your well will stay clean. If you're not careful, you could end up with a very expensive repair bill. Finally, remember that drilling a well is a big commitment. Once you've drilled your well, you're responsible for maintaining it and making sure it continues to provide clean, safe water for your family.

For all these reasons, it's important to weigh the pros and cons carefully before deciding whether or not to drill your own well.

# How to install a hand pump on Your well

Before you even buy a pump, the most critical thing you need to know is how deep the water is below the ground. Without this key piece of information, you run the risk of buying an ill-fitting or incorrect pump for your needs, which could lead to all sorts of problems down the line. Not only will you have wasted your money on the purchase, but you'll also have to deal with the headache of having to install a new pump. To avoid all of this, simply take a measurement of the depth of the water before heading to the store. With this in hand, you can ensure that you're making the right purchase and avoid any costly mistakes.

**How to measure the depth of your well**

While some wells are shallow enough that the water level can be easily seen, others may be hundreds of feet deep. If you need to measure the depth of your well, there are a few different methods you can use. The most common method is to lower a weighted line into the well until it reaches the water. Once the line is in the water, you can simply mark the point where it touches the surface and then measure the length of the line. Another common method is to use a tape measure. Simply attach one end of the tape measure to the top of the well and lower it down until it reaches the water. Again, you can mark the point where it meets the surface and then measure the length of the tape. With either method, be sure to take into account any bends or curves in the well so that you can get an accurate measurement.

**How to install the pump**

Installing a shallow well hand pump is relatively simple and can be done in a few hours. The first step is to connect a length of PVC pipe to the bottom of the pit. The other end of the pipe should be connected to the inlet of the hand pump. Once the pump is in place, secure it with bolts or another type of fastener. Finally, fill the pit with gravel or sand to provide stability for the hand pump. With a little effort, you can easily install a shallow well hand pump that will provide an abundance of fresh water for your home.

**What if you need to install a hand pump for a deep well?**

When it comes to installing a deep-well hand pump, positioning is crucial. The pump needs to be placed at the top of the well so that it can draw water up from the depths below. In addition, the pump needs to be positioned in such a way that it is easy to access and operate. If the pump is too difficult to reach, then it will be of little use in an emergency situation. Positioning is, therefore, an important consideration when installing a deep-well hand pump. With a little bit of planning, you can ensure that your hand pump is both effective and easy to use.

# How to collect grey water

Preppers are always looking for ways to be self-sufficient, and one way to do that is by using grey water. Grey water is the wastewater from household activities like washing dishes, laundry, and showering. It doesn't include water from the toilet or other sources of contaminated water. Grey water can be reused for things like watering plants, flushing toilets, and laundry. It's a great way to save water and money. There are a few things to keep in mind when using grey water:

- Be sure only to collect water that is free of hazardous chemicals, such as bleach or detergent.

- Avoid mixing grey water with black water, which is wastewater that contains human waste.

- Store grey water in a clean, covered container until you're ready

If you're looking for ways to be more self-sufficient, grey water is a great option as long as you filter and purify it. Just be sure to take some basic precautions and you'll be all set!

# CHAPTER 3.
# SELF-SUFFICIENT LIVING

Living off the grid can be a very enticing lifestyle for those seeking more freedom and independence. This means producing your own electrical power, collecting and pumping your own water, and growing your own food. It's not a very common lifestyle. However, many people these days prefer to live independently and to minimize their reliance on fossil fuels. While some people choose to go completely off the grid, others may prefer to go partially off the grid and still rely on the central systems for electricity, gas, or water. There are many advantages to living away from the city. However, not all countries allow this kind of lifestyle. So, here is a self-sufficient living guide to help you get started.

## WHAT IS SELF-SUFFICIENT LIVING?

First, let's go over the definition of self-sufficiency and the main factors contributing to living off the grid. Self-sufficient living is the ability to become the producer and provider for your own daily needs. This includes building or creating your own shelter and getting your own food that may come from the land around you or animals you own. So, one of the main aspects of self-sufficiency is owning a land big enough to hold your home and animals. Another big part of the process is knowing how to maintain your off-grid system and support your home and family. This may also include reaching the required mental stability level that allows you to face large-scale challenges. Doing that will allow you to enjoy the life you have worked to build.

Finally, you need to know how to get yourself out of debt so that all your energy is dedicated to maintaining your off-grid lifestyle. Living out of the city does not require a lot of money, but you still need to save enough for emergencies and put all your money to good use instead of paying interest.

**Getting Rid of Debt**

The first steps you need to take to go off-grid begin when you're still living on-grid. The first thing you need to think of is money, and although you can go off-grid without saving, you first need to work on going debt-free. You also need to accumulate a little bit of cash in order to build a safety net for when you go off-grid. Start by calculating the amount of money you regularly spend every month, then gradually pay off any pending debts before making any preparations. There will always be creative ways by which you can cut expenses and save money. Aim to downsize your requirements and train yourself for living outside the city. Even if it's not to save up and pay off your debts, it's crucial to teach yourself how to live on minimal essentials before making a move.

That being said, let's get into what self-sufficiency is not.

Basically, self-sufficiency is not living as a consumer. You have to rely completely on yourself to provide for your own needs. It's not using dietary staples, animal food, land fertilizers, or any other resources that do not belong to you. Self-sufficiency is not about depending on the grid to let you accomplish your daily chores or tasks. It is also not about self-isolation and turning your back on the community that exists around you. It's more about providing for yourself and knowing that your needs and demands are still met even when community resources cease to exist.

Self-sufficient living does not include depending on purchased canned or dried food without the ability to refill them yourself. So, in a nutshell, self-sufficiency is the physical and mental resilience to all needs. It's about changing your identity and going from a consumer to a producer. While it may be easy to explain in writing, it can be a lifelong journey to understand the concept.

## Off-Grid Living

Apart from the mental and physical aspects of living off the grid, this lifestyle allows you to become less reliant on some principal pillars in the conventional on-grid culture. Let's actually go over them one by one to find out how to substitute them and experience a true self-sufficient lifestyle.

## Electricity

The first and most prominent thing you have to give up when you live off the grid is electricity. You need to be completely independent of the main electric grid. This can be done through various methods. Some people live without electricity, some rely on one or more generators, while others choose to produce their own electricity by depending on alternative energy sources such as the sun or wind.

## Water

Giving up water means disconnecting from the water grid and finding an alternative source that would allow you to build your own water system. Many off-grid homes rely on lakes to provide them with drinking water.

## Natural Gas

This means giving up gas used to heat homes and run stoves.

## Sewer

The sewage system is the part most people forget about before switching to off-grid living. Instead of relying on the main sewer system, you will need to look for an alternative. This includes outhouses, field beds, septic tanks, and composting or propane toilets.

# Advantages of Self-Sufficient Living

### Increased Self-Dependence

One of the best benefits of living off-grid is achieving full self-reliance and learning how to handle yourself in case of societal collapse. You'll learn a great lesson on independence, and you'll be able to master the nature around you. When you live outside of society, you'll be forced to harvest your own food and fulfill your own energy needs, which will teach you to depend on yourself in every aspect.

### More Interaction with Nature

If you are ready with all the necessary all-season equipment and gear, it's guaranteed that you'll enjoy your time outside all year round. Living off-grid is all about spending more time outdoors and connecting more with nature. When you choose this kind of lifestyle, you'll understand how wilderness is the true giver of life. You'll eventually find yourself spending the majority of your time outside, either harvesting food, looking after your land, or simply just relaxing and enjoying the weather.

### Creating an Eco-Friendly Lifestyle

You can make a significant impact on the environment just by switching to an off-grid lifestyle. Think about all the electricity and fossil fuel power you'll be giving up on by disconnecting from the grid. When you switch to self-sufficient living and rely on renewable energy like solar power and wind power for your daily needs, you significantly reduce your carbon footprint and help develop a more sustainable society. You also learn to invest in the best durable gear that is more likely to last for years instead of contributing to the wasteful throwaway culture.

### A More Affordable Lifestyle

While the initial costs of living off-grid can seem a little high, you'll be saving up thousands of dollars in the long run. The initial costs are usually the most expensive since you will need to build a home, set up an electrical system, and invest in durable gear and supplies. Regardless, you'll be saving up a lot of money that could have otherwise been spent on utilities, food, and superfluous expenses.

Now let's take a look at how you'll be able to save money on utilities.

- Solar Power

If you go with solar panels, you'll make a huge positive impact on the environment and save yourself a few thousand dollars every year. Solar power is very affordable now, and it helps homeowners save up a lot on electricity bills. You can actually even use solar panels to cover a small portion of your daily electrical needs while relying on generators for the rest of your power consumption.

- Battery Storage

Battery storage prices are currently coming down to a very affordable level for homeowners. There are many innovative products nowadays, such as the Tesla Powerwall, which is both durable and affordable.

- Electricity Prices

As the current electricity prices are increasing due to many factors such as new grid costs, network infrastructure costs, and the general increase of wholesale electricity prices, you'll be able to save a lot of money if you go off-grid.

# Disadvantages of Self-Sufficient Living

Anything you do will actually have its advantages and disadvantages. However, it's always best to stay prepared for any downfalls you may come across. Here are a few cons of self-sufficient living to keep in mind.

**Initial Costs**

While living off the grid may be one of the cheapest lifestyles, it costs a lot to get started. You'll first encounter the costs of constructing your own home and whatever other utility-alternative systems you need. You'll need to afford your own land and set up a water system for drinking and washing. The gear you buy at the beginning of your switch will also cost you a lot, given that you'll need some long-lasting supplies to help you combat the outdoor environment. It will be quite an investment. Whether you choose a solar power system or any different method, the costs of power will also be quite high. Since cutting these costs won't really be helpful, it would be better to choose your initial investments wisely.

## Roof Space Limitations

Depending on the very specific size of your house, your roof space may not be sufficient for the number of solar panels you need to power your home. In fact, the size of the roof you have over your head is one of the most important determining factors when it comes to meeting your home's electrical needs.

## Reduced Convenience

You'll have to make a few compromises when switching to off-grid living. Let's be honest, there will be no Uber Eats or a fast internet connection. You'll have to get used to the limited access to pharmacies, grocery stores, and even clothes and equipment suppliers. You'll also be disconnected from many professional services such as auto repairs, construction, land management, plumbing, and other common fundamentals.

## Unguaranteed Paybacks

Solar power systems may be affordable at the moment, with acceptable payback periods ranging from 3 to 5 years. However, battery systems are still not a good investment, and their payback periods have only recently been reduced to be shorter than their warranty periods.

## Backup Power Generation

When you go off-grid using solar power, you will need a system that can at least power your home or give you energy autonomy for 3 to 4 days. This means that you'll need a backup generator or battery storage system for emergency situations. Battery storage systems can require a lot of maintenance.

## Property Value

If you're changing to a self-sufficient lifestyle, you need to be prepared for a potential decrease in your property or house value. Some people may be looking forward to buying an off-grid house. However, many other people would look at this fact as a disadvantage rather than a quality. This is why you'll need to make some changes if you're planning to sell your house in the future.

**Loneliness**

Most of the people you actually know probably live in a conventional society. While off-grid communal environments exist, you may not always be lucky to find one or live in one. This is why you need to be prepared to go weeks or even months without talking to anyone. You must be ready for some occasional loneliness if you're really considering self-sufficient living.

**Usage Spikes**

You need to understand that even your regular solar power consumption can be exceeded any day throughout the year. If you have guests over at your house, you're more likely to consume more power than usual. This is why you need to plan your power usage and prepare for unexpected usage spikes.

# Self-Sufficient Living Tips

Now, the previous part may have all been about the difficulties of living off the grid, but apart from the advantages and disadvantages, some tried tips and pieces of advice may help make your life easier when switching to a self-sufficient lifestyle. Here are some of our best tips.

- Adapt to your new home and make your new environment work for you.
- Aim for frugality and living with the available resources or means you're given. You can't expect to switch to self-sufficiency while owing people money and refusing to pay your debts.
- Plan your food according to the season. You won't be lucky enough to rely on grocery stores, so you need to at least eat whatever is in season.
- Aim to create a homestead wherever your home is. This will help you grow your own food and raise the livestock you need to harvest food.

# CHAPTER 4.
# WHY PEOPLE LIVE OFF-GRID?

Some individuals can pursue the off-grid lifestyle for several reasons. Other people want to enjoy money-saving benefits from being disconnected from the public grid. You can live off-grid to have energy security where you may experience power outages in your area. Off-grid power involves electricity that is independent of the council grid and is usually derived from renewable sources.

There are mainly three types of off-grid power generation: wind, solar, and micro-hydro. These energy sources convert their power to direct current electricity in contrast to alternating current supplied by electrical grids. If you are thinking of living off-grid, here are three main types of energy sources you should familiarize yourself with.

# Solar Power

Solar power is by far the most common source of renewable energy used by many people who live off-grid. When you live off the main energy supply, it is cheaper to consider solar power than other sources like generators. When you set an off-grid renewable system, you should minimize your heating and energy use. Using solar energy, you can get enough power for lighting and energy to recharge gadgets like tablets, laptops, and smartphones.

Solar is the most practical energy source since it requires photovoltaic panels that help convert the power from sunlight into electricity. This system requires very few conditions to work, and it can be used in almost all parts of the globe. All you need on top of solar panels is sunny weather. However, during other seasons like winter, a solar system may not be a reliable power source. Additionally, it works perfectly during the day when there is enough sunlight. However, you need to rely on a bank of batteries to store the energy you can use during cloudy days and nighttime.

Battery storage is the heart of different off-grid systems that utilize direct current generated from the sun. With a battery bank, you can store energy generated from the sun and use it when required. Depending on the quality of batteries you choose, the good ones can last up to five years. Lead-acid batteries consist of deep charging cycles and are commonly used on solar systems. To ensure that your power supply is not disrupted, batteries that contain liquid acid require special care.

Absorbent glass mat (AGM) batteries are expensive but easy to look after because they are liquid-free. Besides using solar energy, batteries can also be used to store power produced via multiple-generation technologies.

# Wind Energy

Wind energy is another smart source of electric power. A turbine consists of turbines moved by the wind making the internal generator spin, producing electricity. This electricity is then channeled into the system\, or it can be stored in battery banks. The setup costs for wind generation systems are generally lower than the solar system.

However, when choosing this energy source, you may encounter the challenge that some places don't get much wind. If you live in many tall trees and other physical barriers, wind turbines may not be effective. Another factor is that if your turbine is in a particularly unsteady but windy area, you may not be able to generate a continuous and uninterrupted power supply. Wind turbines require placement in large open spaces to work steadily.

# Micro-Hydro Energy

Micro-hydro energy generation is not very different from wind energy since it uses motion to spin turbines to generate electricity. In this case, water flow is the motion that turns the turbines. As long as there is actually enough water flowing, this method of power generation produces steady electricity. However, the only problem is that investing in this kind of energy generation is costly. It might not be possible to use it for a single household.

# Generators

Generators can actually be used to provide power to people who live off the grid. For instance, if you are not living permanently off-grid, a portable generator can be a good energy source. If you live in a motorhome, you may need a portable generator to meet your energy needs. Big standby generators can also supply energy to homes not connected to the main power supply grid. However, using generators for off-grid power can be costly in the long run. This is the main reason why you can consider the above renewable sources of energy.

# CHAPTER 5.
## GATHERING THE SUPPLIES YOU NEED TO SURVIVE

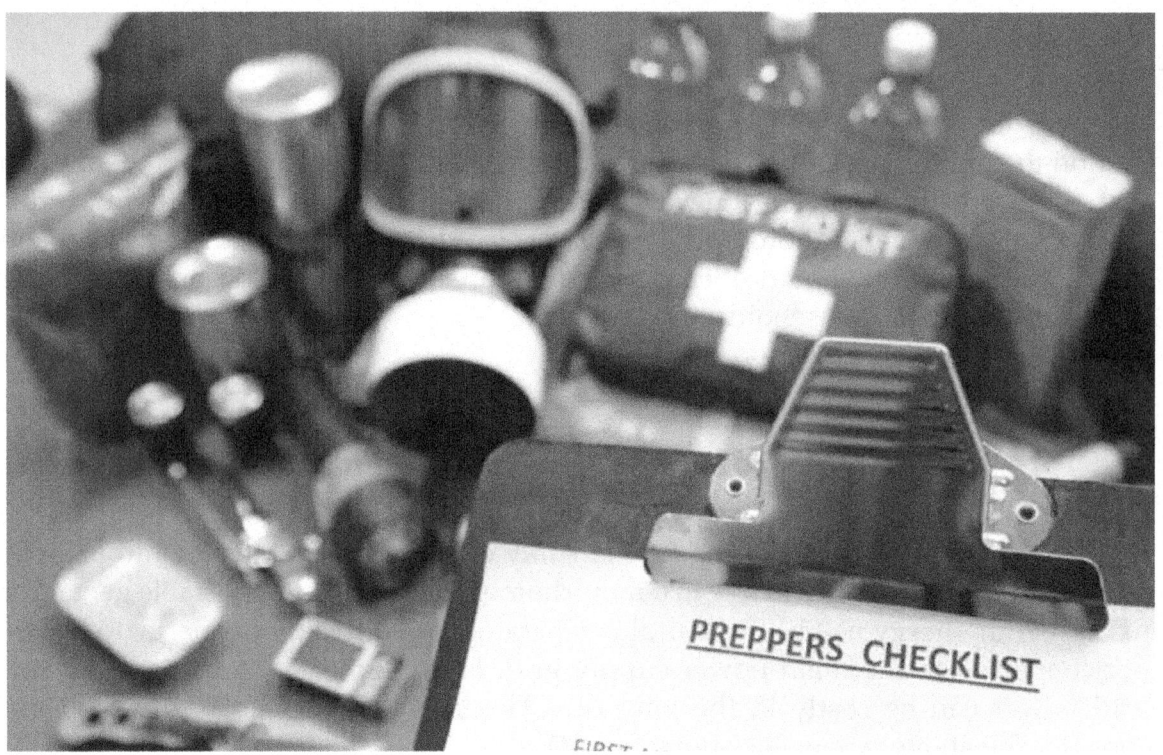

Now that your home is secured, you need to begin to gather the supplies necessary to survive a disaster, whether it be a WROL/AHBL situation or a natural disaster. Before we begin, it's important to note that with a quick internet search, you can find hundreds of prepping supply lists scattered all over the Internet.

The list that follows is not intended to be the most thorough or to be all-encompassing. Its purpose is to give you a list of the most essential, critical items that will ensure that you're able to survive any type of disaster.

In addition, the list does not take extreme living conditions into consideration. However, it will still serve as a good starting point regardless of your dwelling's location. Let's get started.

# SURVIVAL NECESSITIES

### Water / H2O

In a disaster scenario, drinkable water almost immediately becomes the most valuable commodity. Even more so than food because humans can survive longer without food than without water. 60% of the human body is made up of water and the cells that make up our organs need water to keep them working. Water lubricates our joints and keeps our body temperature in check through respiration and sweating. It also helps in eliminating bodily waste.

Water is the universal solvent and is the main indicator that a particular location can support life. In addition to drinking, water is essential for other activities such as bathing, food preparation, and growing crops.

It is extremely important that you stock up on water before a WROL/AHBL situation. It will quickly become difficult to find clean, drinkable water in a disaster scenario. It is also recommended that you have some sort of water filtration system on hand that will allow you to convert non-drinkable water to drinkable. When choosing a water filtration system, choose one that is gravity fed because they offer the best price to performance ratio compared to other water filtration types. If you're alone and portability is of utmost importance, there are some excellent camping water filters available that are small and light-weight enough for you to carry in your backpack or prepper pack.

### Food

The next commodity to begin stocking up on is food. Even though our bodies need water more than food, they still need the nutrients that are only found in food. Nutrient-rich food is necessary to keep our bodies functioning at maximum efficiency. There are four categories that you should consider when stocking up on food supplies. They are short-term, long-term, staples, and ultra-long-term food supplies.

Food is considered "short-term" if it is perishable. Perishable food has a shelf-life of only 30 days or less so you should be sure to consume them before they expire. If you need to extend them past their expiration date, there are ways to preserve them and make them last longer than their designated shelf-life. One example would be sealing them in vacuum sealed jars or bags. It is recommended that you always have a 30-day supply of perishables on hand.

The next food category is "long-term." Food is categorized as long-term if it has an indefinite shelf life. The most common example of long-term food is canned food. Canned tuna, sardines, fruits, chicken, and beans are just some of the examples of canned food. Stock up on this category as much as you are able. In a WROL/AHBL scenario, long-term food will make up the majority of your food stock.

The next category is "staples." Staples are additives that make food taste better or items that allow you to bake or cook better tasting food. Examples of staples would be salt, pepper, spices, baking soda, yeast, flour and sugar. If circumstances allow, stock up on these to expand your food supply. However, these items are not essential to your survival.

Lastly, we have the "ultra-long-term" category. An example of ultra-long-term food is freeze dried goods. The benefits of this type of food are that it doesn't go bad for years, is light-weight, and is easily transported. The downside is that it can be very expensive to buy. Stock up on this type of food if you have plenty of cash and have limited time to prepare.

### Clothing

Your next concern after food and water should be to protect your body against the elements. You should have clothes for both outdoor and indoor use. Clothes can be your last line of defense against the searing heat of summer or the chilling winds of winter. Wicking garments are ideal for the summer and hot climates. Thick garments that you can layer are ideal for winter and cooler climates. It is a good idea to always keep a number of heavy-duty socks and gloves available. In addition, make sure that you have a good pair of sturdy boots to keep your feet protected against rough terrain if you will be traveling.

### Hygiene/First Aid

Hygiene products are very nice to have on hand, but they are not essential. The bare essentials in this category would be something to wash your hands with after touching something dirty or something to scrub your body with when taking a bath. When stocking up on hygienic products think of whether that item would help prevent you from getting sick as you go about your day-to-day activities.

The obvious example of a hygienic item is soap. Soap helps you get rid of the dirt or germs on your body that, if left there, could cause sickness and disease. Another example is hand sanitizer, which helps keep your hands clean during and after you eat or drink.

A good first aid kit is an essential part of your survival supplies. Accidents can occur anytime, anywhere. This is why having a first aid kit handy is extremely important. Small wounds can easily get infected and quickly turn into major injuries. Applying first aid to any injury or wound is a constant necessity. First aid is very often the determining factor in whether someone survives an injury or not.

*Power/Lighting*

Now that you have food, water, clothing, hygienic, and first aid items, the next things that you need to consider are power sources and lighting. It is always best to have an alternative power source in the event the grid goes down. With an alternate power source, you will be able to provide power to the essential tools that you have in order to survive.

Rechargeable batteries can also be extremely useful if the grid goes down. They can power many things like flashlights, radios, GPS devices, etc. If you will be relying on rechargeable batteries, make sure to buy solar-powered battery chargers. They are cheap, readily available, and very user-friendly.

You might also consider keeping old car batteries around as an alternative power source. You can attach a 1000-watt power converter to a car battery and charge small mobile devices and even run small appliances in your home.

If you're going to be in one place for an extended period of time, nothing beats a 3000W power generator as an alternative power source. To keep it running, you will need to stock up on gallons of fuel as well. There is no way to tell how long the grid will go down during a WROL/AHBL scenario so it's a good idea to stock up on fuel whenever possible.

Propane and propane lanterns are also good items to stock up on since they can provide outdoor lighting especially when working in poorly lit areas.

*Tools*

A good rule of thumb is to not buy specialized tools since they don't offer the flexibility that basic tools do. Buy basic, multi-purpose tools as much as possible. Multi-purpose tools are extremely portable and will prevent you from having to bring multiple tools with you while doing repairs. Additionally, tools that can also serve as weapons can be very useful additions to your supply essentials.

*Sanitation Items*

Keeping your living area clean is always important. Therefore, stocking up on sanitation items is a good idea. Trash bags, bleach, and isopropyl alcohol are good examples of items to have on hand for cleaning purposes. Unsanitary conditions can bring about sickness and disease. Keeping your surroundings clean even when the grid goes down is an essential component to survival.

*Communications*

The ability to communicate with the outside world during a crisis or disaster scenario is crucial in mitigating or reducing the damage done to property and life. Essential communication devices include HAM radios and survival-grade "walkie talkies" (two-way radios). Make sure your supplies contain extra rechargeable batteries for these devices.

# SECURITY ESSENTIALS

While the ownership and usage of guns is a controversial topic in the world today, during a WROL/AHBL scenario it is absolutely essential to your safely and survival. You must be able to protect your family, property, and supplies from looters, robbers, or other assailants. A gun is the fastest, safest way to accomplish this. A warning gunshot will go a long way in quickly communicating that you are not someone to mess with. Guns not only act as tools for defense, but they can also be used to hunt game.

Guns and ammunition can be very expensive so it's important that you do your homework before purchasing. It's recommended that you have more than one gun on hand. Handguns or pistols like the 9mm are small, easy to use weapons that are ideal for defending yourself. Rifles are mainly for hunting small game like squirrels, turkeys, etc. but can also be very effective in self-defense. If you have prior firearms experience and want to take your arsenal to the next level, recommendations include a .45 ACP handgun; preferably the Colt 1911 or the 5.56 mm M4 Carbine.

Having the best guns in the world will be of no value to you if you don't have the right ammunition. Stock up on the correct bullets for the guns that you have. Remember, a gun without bullets is just an expensive paperweight.

After purchasing your firearms and ammunition through the proper channels, you should train and practice using them to ensure that you're able to defend yourself safely and effectively.

# Chapter 6.
# Water Procurement

Water procurement and purification play a huge role in living off the grid because you cannot survive without fresh water. You must always be aware of how to find fresh water and purify it when needed so that your chances for survival increase exponentially.

It is important to know where the nearest natural source of water is to avoid having to go too far out of your way. It is also important to know how much water you need per day, which can vary depending on your physical activity levels and the temperature outside.

For example, in extremely hot weather you will need a lot more than usual. The body sweats more in hot weather to cool itself down.

Make sure that you purify all freshwater sources because there could be parasites or microorganisms in them that would make you sick if consumed without proper treatment.

# LOCATING WATER SOURCES

As previously discussed, your shelter should be built near (but not too close) to a water source whenever possible (200 feet away). However, few sources of water are safe for immediate consumption in the wilderness - you may hike up to a clear lake or river and think you've struck gold, but this water can contain millions of organisms (i.e. pathogens, viruses, bacteria, etc.). Depending on the circumstances, drinking water with possible pathogens may be OK if you think a rescue will occur soon. In that case, a hospital will be able to cure any parasites or bacterial infections.

Water flows downhill. Be on the lookout for dips, valleys, and low-lying terrain where water may be flowing. However, avoid any lower elevations you come across (i.e. subalpine areas) because the risk of absorbing harmful pathogens is higher here.

Take note of the vegetation in the area. Any areas with lavish green vegetation are areas where you should be able to find water nearby.

Plants are a water resource. Plants consume water, so they can provide you with a source of water. Strategies for pulling water from plants include consuming the plant itself or extracting the water or sap.

Fruit - For edible sources of water, you can look for fruits such as blackberries or strawberries to readily consume.

Grass - The heavy dew found on grass can also provide readily consumable water:

Tie any absorbent cloth you have available around the shins of your legs, then go for a stroll through the grass before the sun rises to soak up water that can be wrung out for consumption.

**Don't forget to use your senses**

- Rest stops along your trail are great opportunities to observe your surroundings.
- Listen for any signs of water flow/streaming. In the wild, it should not be too difficult to hear, especially in an isolated area.

Most sources will need to be purified before drinking to minimize your risk of illness due to hazardous bacteria or viruses. You should attempt to locate readily-drinkable water first as it will save you time and energy. Your surroundings and the life around the water can indicate where to begin your search for drinkable water.

**Animals need water for survival and know where to go to get safe drinking water**

- Observe wildlife and animal activity to see where they go to get their water.
- Take note of any animal tracks/footprints as they may lead you to sources for available drinking water.
- Birds are also a great guide for finding water:
- Their flight paths can direct you toward a water supply.
- Observe their flight paths, both in the morning and evening, to guide you toward drinkable water in the area.

**Don't forget about the bugs**

- The presence of certain insects can indicate drinkable water sources. Take note of any swarming insects as they typically linger near readily- drinkable water.

**Collect Rainwater**

- Rainwater is a safe, bacteria-free water source.
- Capture the water in containers.
- Direct water into a container with a tarp. Tie the edges of the tarp to high points of a tree or bush and use a rock above the container to create the low point where water will naturally flow.

**Collect Dew**

Dew is a bacteria-free water source.

Soak up the water with a cloth and then squeeze the water out into a container.

# CHAPTER 7.
# GATHERING WATER

Sometimes, there are visible or even liquid sources of water where you are. When this occurs, you will actually have to find another way to gather water. When hiking during winter, you will have access to snow and ice. It is never suggested to consume these, as it will lower your body temperature to dangerous levels. You can build a fire which you can use to melt the solid water. If you cannot start a fire, you can collect it in a bottle, which you can place inside your jacket (but not against your skin) to melt it while you continue to look for shelter.

Although the water doesn't need to be boiled with this method, it is a good idea to filter it because there is a chance of some solid contaminants getting into the water during the collection. There are actually two known ways that you can "create" your own freshwater.

## Method 1

The first is how to get fresh water from saltwater. You can collect saltwater in a pan and bring it to a boil. Once the stream starts to appear, you can add a cloth (or a spare shirt) over the pan. The steam won't contain any of the salt and will condense on the cloth.

## Method 2

A. Start by digging a hole, preferably four feet by three feet down, though this may be dependent on the soil and the size of the plastic sheeting you have available to you.
B. In the center of the hole, add the water collection container. Around this container, add the vegetation, use as many leaves as possible, and don't allow them to be in the container. This vegetation is what will create the moisture in your still.
C. Next, add the sheet over the hole and place rocks around the edge, keeping the sheet in place. Don't allow the sheet to be taut at this point.
D. Add another rock in the center of the sheet, allowing the edges to slope down at a 45° angle.

This isn't your only way to get fresh water from plants and the sun. Through transpiration, you can use a living tree to generate water for yourself.

- Take several plastic bags that can be sealed, with a small, clean stone inside of them, and tie each one over the end of a branch of a tree. Be sure to use a tree that you know is safe.
- When enough liquid has been gathered, remove the plastic bag from the tree and pour its contents into a waiting container.
- As long as the plant is not poisonous, you can drink this water as is, though it is suggested that you filter and boil it just to be safe.

# CHAPTER 8.
# CLEANING WATER

No water supply you come across is going to be completely clean. This is why you should filter and boil any water that you want to drink. Filtering allows you to remove any solid contaminants. Then you will need to boil the water as this will kill the most dangerous microorganisms, such as viruses, bacteria, and parasites.

The first step to cleaning your water is to filter it.

- Add some material on the inside of the bottle, such as grass or fine leaves, and insert these closest to the neck. This will prevent the rest of your filtration pieces from falling out of the bottle.
- You can even add a layer of grass between the sand and the pebbles if available.
- Now you can pour the water you collected through the filtration device.
- The water may have to pass through the filter several times until this happens. If you do not have any bottles, don't fret.

- You can use hollowed-out logs or plants such as bamboo to carry and store your water. Make sure that these have been thoroughly rinsed before they are used.

The next step is to get rid of any microorganisms that may still be in the water.

- To do this, you actually need to boil the filtered water at a rolling boil for no less than one minute.
- After boiling the water, allow it to cool naturally before storing it in a clean container that can be sealed or, at the very least, covered.

# CHAPTER 9.
# PURIFYING WATER

Whether you are storing water for drinking or cooking purposes, the cleaner it is, the longer it will remain fresh. When you remove all the contaminants from the water, including microbes, it is likely to stay fresh for months. For this reason, different purifications are employed. Some of them can be tried at home or in any setting without the use of large-scale machines or equipment, and those methods include:

## BOILING

It is the simplest of the purification methods and also a widely used one. In this method, the water is heated to its boiling point - the temperature at which most microbes cease to exist. Boiling must be employed to filter clean and soft water.

# Water Purifier

Water can also be purified using an electric purifier.

# Reverse Osmosis

This method is a fairly popular one, and there are entire water plants that run to clean water through reverse osmosis. Not everyone can have this technology available at home, so you can simply buy water passed through an RO plant or let your stored water be processed through these plants.

# Water Chlorination

It is not a widely recommended technique, but it can be used to clean the water on an emergency basis. About 5 percent chlorine is added to the water, which then kills the microorganisms. This process is not recommended for drinking water.

# Distillation

Distillation is rather a complex and complicated process, but it gives you the purest of water. It is not as effective as reverse osmosis because it removes all the minerals from the water along with the impurities. It is also time-consuming and cannot be carried out in home settings.

# Solar Purification

The purification technique involves storing the water in food-grade plastic bottles, then shaking them well to activate the oxygen. Then, the bottles are kept in sunlight horizontally. By doing so, the viruses and bacteria are killed due to the UV rays.

# Chapter 10.
# Storing Water

It might be hard to find clean water after an uncommon tragedy, and it may contaminate your regular drinking water source depending on its consequences and intensity. Prepare for an emergency by storing a supply of water that will meet the needs of you and your family members. Managing water and the way to keep it safe rely on the type of emergency. Few ways and facilities may ease you to save your water and have clean water. Bottled water is one of the best options you can choose.

Following calculations are based on experiences and observations set by physicians and biologists as a recommendation.

If there is anyone with you who is expected to get sick, or a pregnant woman, you should consider storing more water than the above-recommended calculation. Also, consider the climate situation. If it's hot, it will cause trouble for your stored water and increase drinking demand.

When using containers to safely treat your store water for use and keep it drinkable, it is best to use food-grade storage containers that do not allow the transference of toxic substances into the water. FDA (Food and Drug Administration) approved food-grade storage containers can be easily found at camping supply stores or web stores.

## Has Tightly-Closed Cap

It is required to have a cap that can tightly close and hold water when there are bumps and jumps. It should be made of durable, unbreakable materials; glass materials are futile in such situations, so those are not ideal. Use a container with a narrow opening so water can be poured out.

## New Containers

It is highly prohibited to use containers that have been previously used to hold liquid or solid toxic chemicals, such as bleach and pesticides.

## Pouring Water

Precautions should be taken for removing safe water out of the container, otherwise you'll contaminate your container and the water. If using a scoop or pot, clean it before and after pouring out water from your container to avoid contamination of all the water. Be sure not to touch the container's water surface and walls with your hand or another thing while pouring water. Never pour out safe water using your hands.

## Safety Tips

If you are storing water for an extended period of time, it's crucial to use a container that seals tightly and is made of food-grade plastic. It should be marked "Drinking Water" and sanitized, so it doesn't retain contaminants.

Then, rinse the container thoroughly with clean water. When you're finished, pour out the solution and air-dry it. If you're using a scoop, make sure it's clean for each scoop. It's best to use clean hands when scooping the water, and you should never touch the container or the water. Once it's clean, you can use it to store clean water. Usually, you should replace this water every six months.

There are several methods for disinfecting water. The first method is the simplest and cheapest. Boiling water at 100 degrees Celsius for at least 20 minutes kills most bacteria and pathogenic organisms. Once the water cools, transfer it into a clean container. Another method involves oxygenating water by pouring it between two clean containers. The oxygen in the water will improve its taste.

To avoid the risk of bacteria or microbial contamination, plastic containers should be FDA-approved. Specifically, polyethylene plastics are FDA-approved for water storage. If a container is not FDA-approved, it might contain harmful chemicals that leach into water when used.

Another option for safe water storage is storing it in the freezer. This is useful in times when the power is out. If you are storing water in the freezer, plastic containers are ideal. Glass containers may not withstand the pressure from expanding ice. For safety purposes, the container should be stored high and out of reach of pets and children. Whenever you fill a container with water, use it within a day or two. Once you've cleaned and sanitized the container, you need to make sure that you've stored enough water in it. Usually, the average person needs about a gallon of water per day for drinking, brushing their teeth, and minimal dish washing. To be extra safe, you can invest in an emergency water heater that can supply up to 80 gallons of water if necessary.

# Chapter II.
# Preserving Your Water

Water must be stored correctly so that it does not become contaminated. It must be preserved for longer-term storage or small microbes can breed and cause illnesses that can lead to even more serious medical conditions. If you are storing tap water, you may not need to add anything to it because most cities add chlorine as part of their system anyway.

If you are actually using any other type of water for longer term storage, you will need to add bleach or iodine. Use bleach for stored water and iodine for possibly contaminated drinking water at the point of use.

# CHLORINE

There are several ways to add chlorine to your water for storage so that it is safe when you are ready to drink it. The simplest is to use liquid bleach, making sure that you are using the type listed as 5.35% chlorine content without any additives or scents. This will kill virtually all of the bacteria that could potentially cause illness.

To do so: add two drops of the liquid bleach to each two quarts of water you are storing. At this point, you should smell the chlorine but if you do not, you may need to add slightly more. Start with another drop to two drops and that should do the trick.

When you are ready to drink this water, open the container and let it stand for thirty minutes or more. (You may need to leave it stand opened for 45 minutes or more if you added the additional drops of bleach.)

Chlorine must be stored at temperatures that are fairly stable and never go below fifty degrees or above seventy. You should note that the bleach will start to degrade after one year. Chlorine that is listed as 6% sodium hypochlorite will degrade even faster and must be replaced after three months.

# CALCIUM HYPOCHLORITE

An even better option than liquid bleach is called calcium hypochlorite or its more common term, "pool shock". This has a longer shelf life and can treat more water as well. You can buy this in two forms, the dry and the hydrated.

The hydrated is safer for the average person to handle but the dry can be stored for virtually forever. You must find the pool shock that is 68-78% calcium hypochlorite without any additives like water softeners (may be listed as anti-scaling agents on the label).

To use the pool shock for water storage, you must create a treatment solution first.

***DO NOT DRINK THIS SOLUTION!***

Be sure to carefully label the solution with the proper warnings and instructions for usage. The solution will be one teaspoon of the shock to every two gallons of water.

When you are storing the water, you use the solution in a ratio of 1 to 100 – one part of the solution to every 100 parts of the water you are storing.

Again, do not drink the storage solution. Used in this way, a single pound of pool shock will effectively treat as much as ten thousand gallons of water.

# IODINE

Iodine is more effective than bleach at killing giardia lamblia which can cause giardiasis. It is also better for use as a treatment for water that you are about to drink rather than as a storage treatment. Iodine should be used for water if you are not sure of its source or how it was stored.

It works best in warmer temperatures and the bottle must be stored away from direct light. Iodine should always be kept in a dark colored, glass bottle.

There are several cases where iodine may not be helpful or should not be used. Anyone who is allergic to shellfish is at a higher risk of being allergic to iodine as well. Women who are actually over the age of fifty as well as anyone who is or may be pregnant, people who have known thyroid conditions or are taking the medication lithium should speak to a doctor before using iodine.

Portable aqua water treatment tablets should be included in the bug out bag as an emergency backup.

# CHAPTER 12.
## MANAGING WATER RESOURCES

Water is an irreplaceable natural resource. It's important to actually drink enough water on a daily basis, and not just because it makes up approximately 60% of your body. Water also plays an important key role in the transportation of nutrients into your blood stream, detoxification of bodily toxins, flushing out impurities and waste products from your body, and much more. Without water for these purposes however, you could have a variety of health problems that may not show any outward signs in the form of visible symptoms. A great example of this is a condition known as hyponatremia (low blood sodium), which has caused the deaths of numerous athletes during endurance sports such as marathon running.

The body requires a certain amount of water in order to perform basic life-sustaining functions such as circulation, digestion and various biochemical processes. But we people have created a "modern" lifestyle that often ignores this fact and results in most people not drinking enough water on a daily basis.

Sufficient amounts of the right kind of water are essential for good health, because our bodies can't produce it by themselves.

Since water makes up 60% of our weight, we need adequate quantities every day to survive. On average, men should drink 3.7 liters of water every day, and women need to drink 2.7 liters. Of course, it actually varies from person to person depending on gender, body size, climate and level of physical activity. Since our water intake mostly comes from the food we eat (60%), the quality of water we consume is equally important as the quantity of water we consume. The Food & Agriculture Organization (FAO) has established guidelines for drinking water quality in its publication "Guidelines for Drinking-Water Quality" (1987). Not all waters are equal!

# Water Purification Techniques

The quality of water will vary dramatically depending on the quality of the source. If the water runs through a crack in the sidewalk or near an old gas station, it may contain lead or other pollutants. Once these chemicals are in our drinking water, they pose serious health risks, including genetic mutations and cancer.

The most common filtration technique involves using chemical additives that kill harmful bacteria and other microorganisms to prevent waterborne diseases. Water that has been purified can then be considered to be safer for drinking. Some filters, such as activated carbon filters, remove chemicals from the water like chlorine and lead from pipes, while others remove bacteria from contaminated sources like lakes or rivers.

There are both industrial, and household uses for water purification throughout history. The ancient Egyptians developed a method of purifying saltwater used in their rituals by absorbing light energy at particular angles through a prism called a Harshan prism. The ancient Greeks and Romans utilized contact lenses made of gold to purify the water and bronze to run water through it.

Modern methods for household use include filters, chemicals, boiling, distillation, and ultraviolet light. The latest research in studying the interaction between molecules and light has allowed scientists to develop new methods that are less expensive, energy-efficient, environmentally friendly, and are more effective at removing harmful microorganisms from contaminated waters.

To make pure drinking water, first, the water must be treated to eliminate any harmful microorganisms and bacteria by filtering it through activated carbon filters or other chemical filters. Another method is boiling the $H_2O$ in place: this can be done in an open vessel or with special-purpose equipment.

Next, the water should be disinfected. This process will kill any remaining microorganisms in the water. There are multiple methods for killing these bacteria, including chlorination, UV radiation, or adding an appropriate amount of hydrogen peroxide to the water. For example, two drops of 3% hydrogen peroxide ($H_2O_2$) per liter of water will kill all bacteria and viruses in that volume of tap water in a laboratory environment.

Next, any chemicals in the water should be removed by adding a desalination filter to the end of the purification system. Waters with high salts, nitrates, or metals are usually not potable without removing these harmful chemicals.

Finally, after filtering and disinfecting, the water must be treated with chemicals for taste and odor, if necessary. This step is optional. For example, chlorine alone is sufficient to treat their home water supply, but some prefer to add hydrogen peroxide or sodium bicarbonate.

In general, UV radiation treatments are the most energy-efficient and environmentally friendly method of purification. Organic molecules such as DNA have a peak sensitivity at around 250 nanometers (nm). This means that UV radiation at wavelengths between 200 and 270 nm is most likely to damage DNA.

However, UV radiation can be used for purifying small amounts of water only. To treat larger volumes of water, the flow rate needs to be reduced, and the UV source needs to be closer to the water, which effectively limits production capacities.

Manual filtration can be performed using cloth (like a towel), paper filter, or even sand and gravel. The effectiveness of these filtrations depends on the size of the particles that they can catch. It also depends on how fast or slow the water is passing through these filters. If it's too slow, the filter might get clogged with larger particles than intended for it to catch; if it's too fast, lots of smaller particles might pass through undisturbed (see Micron).

Chemical Water Treatment (CWT) is a more advanced technique for cleaning up contaminated water. It is usually performed in conjunction with boiling or other filtration methods, mainly because it has a significant role in reducing the total amount of chemicals that have made their way into the water. CWT is also sometimes done in place of boiling if there are no other options. There are several different CWT techniques, and each one has its unique pros and cons. The most common CWT units for potable tap water are activated alum (AA) and carbon filters (CF). These filters remove most metals such as lead, arsenic, copper, iron, and manganese. Some of the activated alum units also release some volatile organic compounds (VOCs). Carbon filters are not effective for ion exchange, but they can remove VOCs, pesticides, organic compounds, radon, and even bacteria. Some carbon filters also contain silver ions, which kill bacteria and viruses.

Boiling water is a common technique used in the developing world to make it safe for consumption. This process is also relatively inexpensive, although fuel required for heating water could be costly in remote areas. One boiling water method is to boil the water in a container and then let the steam condense back into the water. The disadvantage to this method is that there can be a considerable cooling time between the boiling and condensing stages. Another approach is to heat water but does not let it boil. This works best for small batches of 1-2 gallons since it takes longer for larger volumes of water.

Several conventional filtration methods are used in urban areas to remove pathogens and particulate matter from drinking water, including activated alumina (AA), carbon filters, ceramic filters, membranes, and sand filtration. However, it's important to actually note that these methods have their limitations and are not without their own set of problems.

# Purifying Water for Cooking and Drinking

The water we drink, cook with, and use in cleaning is an essential resource to our health.

Purifying your drinking water will significantly reduce the risk of getting sick from harmful contaminants. There are also some ways you can cleanse your cooking and washing water that doesn't require chemicals or fuel.

The more people, the more water needed.

Collect all the equipment you'll need to purify and store your water before beginning the process of filtering out contaminants through boiling and other methods.

People who do not have training in microbiology or toxicology should never attempt to purify water of this nature and seek out an alternative source for water immediately.

If there is time available, allow contaminated tap or river water just enough time to settle before collecting it to reduce potential sediment in your container from flowing into your pot or container as you contain its contents.

The most critical part of purifying your drinking water is to boil it, killing all the bacteria living in it. If you cook your water, the water will also taste fresher.

However, some of these methods may take several days to complete. Other methods can be used to purify water, such as filtering quickly. If you can only boil your water for a short period or do not have the materials available to filter it, boiling and filtering can still work.

The first step to purifying water from a natural source is collecting the water yourself. The fewer people that touch the water before it is filtered, the cleaner the final product will be. If you have no container, try to find one that has not been cleaned to minimize the amount of contamination coming in contact with your pitcher or cup. Use clean containers, cups, and utensils as much as possible for this exact reason. If an item cannot be found that has not been cleaned, try to use a container that has an interior that is only one part, with no crevices where bacteria or dirt can hide. Use a halogen or heat source for maximum sterilization.

If the water you collect from a natural source moves slowly enough to allow sediment to settle out of the water before collection, then try to let it sit as long as possible before collecting. The less deposit you have to filter out of your drink, the better. If there is no time to let the water sit before collection, try scooping up water that has sat still to avoid stirring up sediment.

Using one method or a combination of procedures for purifying drinking water as described above, individuals can ensure that they are consuming safe drinking water and do not risk become ill from disease-causing agents such as e-coli, hepatitis A and salmonella.

# Chapter 13.
# Mistakes that Preppers Need to Avoid

Prepping isn't easy to do, and as a beginner, you are likely to make many mistakes. You can scare yourself to death reading everything you find on the internet about prepping, especially when people talk about things that went wrong. However, proper preparation and attention to detail mitigate most risks – you cannot account for everything, but you can certainly reduce the potential for things to go wrong.

To that end, here are **the top 15 mistakes that you should avoid making**:

### 1. Keep Your Mouth Shut! Do Not Tell Others About Your Emergency Shelter

Have you ever watched "Shelter Skelter", an old The Twilight Zone episode? Find it on YouTube and watch it – it will tell you why you should keep your mouth shut. In short, a man at a party shoots his mouth off about his emergency shelter. Then, when the emergency sirens go off, every one of his neighbors turns up at his door, smashing the shelter door off. It turns out that it was a false alarm, but if it happened to you and the cause was an atomic blast, you would have received a huge dose of radiation.

The only people you should tell are those that you trust 100 percent and that you want joining you in your shelter should the need arise. The only other people you can talk to it about are other preppers if you have a community near your home. Other than that, keep it zipped and tell no one else.

Desperate people are the most dangerous, and the last thing you need is desperate people trying to get into your last safe place.

## 2. Not Doing Your Disaster Scenario Homework

Some disasters are common in certain areas, and the biggest mistake you can make is not prepping for what is common in your area. It's fine if you've prepped for all potential scenarios, but if you, for example, prep for the worst case, such as nuclear fallout, and not for tornadoes that are common in your area, then you're going to be out of luck when the next one hits.

Say that your area is prone to severe flooding every ten years or so. You might think that ten years is a long time and the last one only happened two years ago – you've got plenty of time, right? Wrong. With global warming and the crazy weather patterns of late, another flood could happen at any time. And if you're not actually prepared for it, you could be in serious trouble.

Obviously, you don't want an underground shelter in a flood scenario – you will lose the lot. And what if you live in a hurricane-prone area? You may not have to leave your home, but you should be prepared for water, gas, and electricity supplies to fail, at least for a few days. You also need to be prepared for the temperatures – a disaster can strike at any time, be it the height of summer and or in the depths of a frozen winter.

## 3. Not Staying in Shape

As a prepper, you actually need to be ready for anything, and that means staying in shape. You cannot possibly protect yourself, your family, and your property if you can't even make it up one flight of stairs without collapsing at the top.

You live in a fast, busy world, and there isn't always enough time to work out. And then there's the expense of a gym membership to consider. Well, you don't have to join a gym to get in shape. Start working out at home instead. There are actually plenty of specific exercises you can do in just five minutes at home. And if you take public transport to work, get off at an earlier stop and walk the rest of the way. Take the stairs, not the actual escalator or elevator; go for a half-hour walk at lunchtime. So many things you can do, and it all adds up to a fitter, more prepared you. And if your family needs to get in shape too, head out for bike rides and hikes on the weekends.

### 4. You Don't Have any Training or Survival Skills

It's all very well splashing out on expensive survival gadgets and spending a fortune on prepping – which you don't have to do –, but you also need to learn the necessary skills to use such gadgets to the best effect. Buy whatever you think will work, but take the time to learn how to use it in the event of an SHTF scenario.

Think about it; you get caught out in a crisis, you don't have your bug-out bag with you or any weapons for self-defense. Or you do, and you don't know how to use them. What then? You could rely on yourself to a certain extent, but without survival skills and training, you won't last long in the face of danger.

Provided you are in good shape, learned self-defense, and have a variety of survival skills under your belt, you actually have a much better chance of surviving pretty much any disaster situation. You don't have to be Bear Grylls, but you do need some skills.

### 5. Not Choosing the Right Foods for Long-term Storage

You might think any old dried or canned food will do, and there are some strange items that you might see on survival videos that really are not suitable items to stockpile. Take Ramen noodles or Ramen soups – there is more nutrition in a cardboard box! They are not healthy and are full of salt, and unless you have several liters of water spare to wash it down – which you won't have –, you won't last long living on them. Plus, they contain no protein and no other nutritional value.

You must check the labels on the food you store. Too many people pack their kits full of high-sodium snacks – while it is nice to have the odd treat, that's not what this is about. Concentrate on ensuring you store foods with a balance of protein, fat, and carbohydrate – these are the essential macronutrients for health. Having a few salty snacks on hand is fine, but don't go overboard – be sure to do your research before you buy emergency food stores on the internet.

### 6. You Have Too Many Small Pets

This could be a controversial point. Most people prep for natural disasters and smaller-scale disasters, those that could leave them with no power or water for days or longer, and in these cases, a couple of smaller animals is fine. If you are actually one of those that believes the apocalypse is just around the corner, though, and you must have an animal, get a bigger one.

Large dogs can help protect you when you are trying to survive, while smaller animals will drag you down.

### 7. Forgetting to Have Something to Exercise Your Mind

Whether you actually bug in or bug out, you need to have something to keep your mind ticking over. While food and water are important for survival, don't neglect your mind. Put some books in your stockpile, a mixture of genres, and don't forget to include a few survival books too – these will be of great benefit in an SHTF scenario. Put away books on creating a garden, food preservation, first aid skills, and anything else you can think of that will help in a desperate situation.

You should also store a few board games, packs of cards, puzzle books, and other fun things that will keep you occupied and stop your brain, turning to mush.

### 8. You Don't Have Fitness Gear in Your Emergency Shelter

This doesn't refer to "the big stuff", like running machines and so on, but you should have some kind of exercise equipment. Not only will it keep your fitness levels up, but research also shows that exercise can stop you from becoming depressed.

All you need is actually a few dumbbells, a set of resistance bands, and any other small fitness equipment you can think of. That type of gear can even go with you if you need to bug out.

### 9. You Have Far Too Much Reliance on Electronics

How many prepper videos have you seen where people bury items and then mark them on their GPS? You might think that's a great idea, but what happens if the grid goes down? What happens if a massive electromagnetic pulse (EMP) bursts in your area? That's right, your GPS won't work, and you won't find where you buried your gear.

Do things the old-fashioned way – learn how to read and use a map. People do still use them; not everyone relies on a GPS to get them where they need to go. Invest in a map showing your area and a bit wider out if necessary. You can also invest in a map book, showing the whole country. That way, you can get where you need to go without relying on a GPS.

You should also learn to navigate by the sun and stars – it's not as hard as you think. You can also purchase a small Faraday cage or Faraday bag that will keep your electronics safe in the event of an EMP.

### 10. You Spend Far Too Much on Survival Gadgets

This is another major mistake by prepper beginners. You start surfing the Net, looking for survival gear, and you get sidetracked by expensive, unnecessary gadgets. How many variations of a knife have you seen? How many different axes or flashlights? At the end of the ay, you should keep it simple. Buy only what you really need and leave the gadgets to someone else. Set yourself a monthly budget and don't go over it.

### 11. You Don't Monitor Expiry Dates

You should always have actual water purification tablets on hand and two types of food storage – near future and far future. For the latter, make sure you check expiry dates and rotate your stock regularly. When you buy items, stick an expiry label on it and have things stored in order of their date – this also applies to your water containers, as water will go bad if not stored properly or it gets contaminated in some way. Your water purification tablets will help if your water goes green, so make sure you have plenty of them and that they are always in date.

### 12. Failing to Stay Organized

It's one thing to ensure you have adequate food stock, but storing it in a room and then forgetting about it is not good practice – by the time you need it, it may no longer be edible.

You should actually also plan for the eventuality that you may need to evacuate – not just your home but your town or city. Make sure you have a bug-out plan in place that gives you a fast, safe way out, avoiding huge traffic tailbacks.

### 13. You Don't Have Enough Water

Most preppers aim for 72 hours' worth of food, but water is a different matter. You might think a couple of cases will do the trick, but it won't. You have to consider at least two liters of water per person per day for drinking, more if the temperatures are high. Then factor in cooking and washing, and you can see it starts to add up. The minimum is a gallon per person per day – bear in mind that you can go for three weeks without food but actually only three days with no water – make it your top priority.

### 14. Planning to Bug Out and Not Bug In

Many preppers focus on scenarios where they have to evacuate their homes and travel into the woods to bug out. But not all scenarios require that; when earthquakes or hurricanes strike, the best place you can be is in your basement, safe at home.

At the end of the day, bugging in is always going to be better than bugging out, but few preppers even consider it and don't bother making a plan. Clearly, you need to focus on a bug-out plan because the implications are more serious, but never neglect a plan to stay at home for a few days.

### 15. Keeping Your Prepping Gear Together in One Place

Another common rookie mistake is storing everything in the same place. It might seem sensible, but really, it isn't. For example, say that you store everything in your garage. When a hurricane hits, your garage is the weakest point – what if you can't get into it to get all your gear out? Spread your gear around your home, so at least some of it is accessible should the need arise. You could even consider a rented storage locker for some stuff – that way, if you are out and can't get back to your home, you at least have access to something you can use.

# CONCLUSION

Now it is time to actually start applying all this knowledge to your particular situation and become water secure. To avoid paralysis of analysis, take small actions first. Take an easy action first so you get the satisfaction that comes from moving forward on a plan. Go out right now and build up a few weeks emergency water stash.

Then work to make your storage program more robust. Research and purchase a water treatment system that is right for you. Or look at large storage containers that could work in your home. Or start planting a water garden. Build on your program day by day and you will soon have a bulletproof water program that will actually keep your family safe and healthy through any emergency.

When you find tutorials that are useful to you, print them out and keep them in a preparedness folder for reference when you need them.

Living off-grid can be challenging since you will be detached from the modern world. However, as you have observed in this book, it does not necessarily mean that you will lead a primitive lifestyle.

This guide mainly focused on enlightening people who want to live off-grid about the basic survival skills to improve their experience away from public utilities. Living away from the hectic city life may not be for everyone, but it is one of the best ways to enjoy nature.

This book explains the essential steps to creating a sustainable life wherever you go. You must learn to create your own shelter and live independently without technology away from a traditional house. To live comfortably, you must also grasp water and waste management.

This booklet will help you prepare for life without power, running water, technology, or grocery shops. This book actually covers all you need to know to travel the globe and live off-grid.

Our purpose is to educate you how to survive in an emergency. With the correct information and techniques, you can conquer any obstacle. The booklet also provides safety recommendations for handling perilous circumstances.

This survival book includes instructions on catching rainwater, producing food, building heat sources, and rearing animals. A typical existence apart from contemporary culture is covered in this book. Living off-grid has numerous benefits, but it is not always the case. So, here's all you need to know about living without running water or power.

Off-grid may conjure up images of living in the wild, but it's not the same. You can construct a traditional house, but you will lack power from the main grid. Learning about off-grid life is essential if you want to enjoy it.

As you can see, this lifestyle requires excellent DIY abilities. The book emphasizes the need of learning various survival techniques. So, if you wish to live off-grid, this manual has all the information and tools you need.

It provides you with useful abilities to deal with any scenario.

If you wish to live off-grid, this book may help you learn all you need to know. Living off the grid entails fundamental life skills, sourcing food, creating sustainable water sources, and other necessities.

Get this well-researched manual today and start your quest.

# WATER BATH CANNING & PRESERVING COOKBOOK FOR PREPPERS

A TASTY COLLECTION OF OF HIGH-PROTEIN RECIPES AND EFFECTIVE METHODS TO PRESERVE FOODS, BUILD A FAMINE-PROOF PANTRY AND LIVE OFF-GRID

Reed Parker

# TABLE OF CONTENTS

# INTRODUCTION

H ave you ever tried canning food at home? Do you want to end your reliance on expensive market-bought canned food, wouldn't it be nice if you could stay in your home, surviving off your food pantry supplies while you comfortably wait for things to settle down?

Of course, it would be! This is why a survival pantry should be a top priority for every household. Canning is a method of preserving foods by storing them in containers, or jars, which are then securely sealed and sterilized by high heat over a set period of time.

Canning is a simple, inexpensive, effective, and safe process used to preserve food without adding chemicals or other additives. Microorganisms can be destroyed at normal boiling temperatures when highly acidic food has the lowest pH value. But when the food is considerably less acidic, extremely high boiling temperatures are needed to destroy the microorganisms. This is why canning works better for preservation than the normal boiling or cooking technique. In canning, both the pH and temperature of the food are optimized to prevent spoilage through bacterial or fungal growth. In this way, the food remains preserved for a longer duration.

In the event of a major world calamity, it is likely that virtually all commercial canning and food processing plants will cease operation. Without food that has been sealed properly, most foods will be contaminated and go bad within days or a few weeks. But as long as the food is properly canned at normal boiling temperatures, it will maintain its taste and nutritional value for up to two years or more.

This makes it a very good idea to organize your time and produce in an orderly fashion. Practising canning is similar to the assembly line fashion. For canning to work best, your workspace must be organized.

The number of jars you need depends on the food you choose to can. For example, most people recommend canning jars holding from ½ to 1 litre of food. How much food you want to store will depend on how many people in your family and how many jars you can produce.

The basic steps in canning are:

Pick the food to can. Wash and peel it, if required. Pat it dry. Prepare the jars that will hold your food. Fill them with your food. Take care to follow the directions in the canning recipe precisely. Seal each jar with a lid and a blow-off cap.

Preparing the jars is the most difficult part of canning.

There are two types of lids for jars: the conventional plastic screw-on lid and the canning lid. The conventional plastic lid is much more common. It is the easiest to obtain, and its use tends to be more accepted. However, it can be difficult to find these lids in stores, particularly if you live in an area lacking in supermarkets or in an urban area where parts of it are still covered by snow.

The canning lid fits right into the canning jar -- it has a rubber ring on the underside of it that holds it securely in the jar. (If you can't find a canning lid, substitute a replacement plastic lid. Or, instead of a canning lid, you can use two to three inches of water in a salt-water solution and submerge the jar into the solution.

For an extended shelf-life, place two to three inches of water in a quart canning jar and submerge the jar in cold water for a few minutes. The warm, moist air inside the jar encourages the growth of microorganisms that can survive without air.

Next, you must sterilize your canning jars by washing them in hot water and rinsing them very cleanly. Then, it is important to dry the jars completely and set them aside. Turn the jars upside down and let them sit on newspaper until they are completely cool to the touch.

The final part of the packing process is to remove the food particles that have become trapped between the sides of the jars. Press down and away from the jar (with clean, dry hands). Then remove the rings, lightly tap the jar on the counter several times, and rinse the jar under hot running water.

It is unnecessary to clean and dry the lids: they should be packed, too. They can be stored on the counters of your kitchen or stored in a safe, clean place in your pantry, basement, or utility room.

The required processing time can be difficult to calculate because most of the water has boiled away, but it is even more critical that the processing time be kept to the shortest time possible without pulverizing the food.

Finally, store the food in your refrigerator for four days to allow any new bacterial spores to avoid. After four days in the fridge, the food should be safe to eat.

Many people think canning is done using the same tools and recipes as cooking: Use a pot and dish and a lid, right? In reality, canning is done using a world of tools and tools designed especially for canning food.

Besides the regular kitchen tools, you need special ones like canning tongs and a rack; you also need a canning funnel and canning jar lifter. No matter how well you organize your kitchen, these tools may not be available.

# CHAPTER I.
## WHY SHOULD YOU PRESERVE FOOD?

Food preservation is a skill that could save your life. Many people think preparing food for storage and long-term preservation is too much trouble. Others think they have no storage space. Here are some reasons why you should invest some time in learning how to store food:

■ It's inexpensive: Even if food quality and prices go up, you will be saving money by not overeating at a time when costs are going up. Hunger is a natural reflex, but it occurs more often when other things in life are out of control. In the long run, you will save money and help the economy.

■ It's a skill: Saving food is a form of self-defence because you can boost your food supply by reducing your intake of that big volume of food. Learn how to store food and you will be prepared should a natural disaster or some other unforeseen calamity occur.

■ It's good for you: A balanced diet is the best insurance against serious illness. Think about how many healthy foods you can store. If a big hoarder of food like a rat comes in, you would have food for everyone.

■ It's fun: Try different recipes and plan your meals to save time and money.

■ It's a hobby: Food storage is a hobby that can hone your survival skills and make you more confident in any survival situation. People who store food for emergencies also depend on geographical redundancy. Learn about saving food because it benefits you, your family, and society.

■ It's for emergencies: War, floods, earthquakes, and hurricanes have worldwide coverage, and you can't just 'turn them off. Social breakdown causes trouble and knowing how to store food is a sure way to survive economic disasters. You will have food to eat, but others might not.

■ It enables you to be self-sufficient: The real backup of a survivalist is that you can do things for yourself. It's a matter of self-reliance to make things better for yourself. Knowing how to store food for emergencies is a skill nobody can take from you.

■ It's flexible: To stock up on good food for emergencies requires planning for the future. Many people think storing food would mean 'preparing for the apocalypse', but you can save food for emergencies. You can eat it while you're putting food away.

Having a full pantry means being more prepared for food shortages. Food storage can turn you from being a victim to a provider of essential elements that normal people take for granted.

## Tips for Storing Food

To prepare for a disaster, you must start by building a food storage and backup plan. Storing food is an essential part of a prepared individual. Without food, you are at the mercy of an emergency situation.

Here are some tips for food storage:

■ High-quality foods, such as food preserved by canning, freezing, or dehydrating, are the most practical method to store food. Some survivalists believe that keeping foods safely in an underground bunker and preparing some meals also helps you maintain your sanity in the hardest of times.

■ Take care in choosing storage containers. Food storage supplies are the most important things in a disaster, and you must prepare for this kind of disaster beforehand.

■ A storage space is important as it determines how much food you can store and what foods you can store. ⅓ to ½ of the internal space of a building is sufficient for storing food.

■ Always maintain good record keeping. Recognize the relationship between food quantity and storage space. The unit sometimes matters in the food storage business, and you must revise your list of supplies every three months.

■ Evaluate your food storage program and check your food storage inventory at least once a year.

■ Don't eat from your food storage. It is an important key to successful storage. Food storage is a great expense if your goal is to survive the toughest times.

■ Include a few comfort foods in your food storage, though they may be expensive. These foods can be used when you are celebrating or need a pick-me-up.

■ Create a stockpile of long-lasting foods such as salt, sugar, and wheat.

■ Replace the old food with new food in your pantry. Ideally, you should rotate your food at the end of each year.

■ Use a rotation system to organize your food storage. The original contents of the storage space are marked at the front of the storage space when it is explored.

■ Water storage: Always ensure you have water in your storage space. Water is essential for cooking, boiling water, and drinking, too.

# Chapter 2.
# How Canning Works?

## Home Canning Methods

There are two methods of home canning:

### 1. Water Bath Canning Method:

Water bath canning is actually a method of preserving food in a water bath. This is a lower-temperature canning technique that's great for high-acid foods & recipes with the right amount of acid. Fruits, jellies, jams, salsa, pickles, tomatoes, chutneys, sauces, pie fillings, & condiments are all good candidates.

### 2. Pressure Canning Methods:

Canning is a process of preserving food with air and water in a sterile environment. It stores food items such as fruits, vegetables, meat, fish, and more to extend their shelf life up to many months or even years. The process is often done in a huge pressure canner, usually made of steel. This can be expensive, but it can keep your food storage items safe and fresh. You can save money if you purchase a reusable canning kit and put it in your pantry for food storage.

There are many pressure canning methods to choose from. If you have an old pressure cooker that regularly gets used for canning your food, then you can just start preserving food using this method. Some old pressure cooker owners have resorted to putting an old timer chicken egg timer on top of the cooker to serve as a warning timer for canning. This is because most old pressure cookers have a steam regulator valve that will not allow more steam to be released once it has reached a certain volume, preventing overcooking of the food items inside. Nowadays, pressure cookers come with built-in canning regulators, which allow processing and canning of the food inside without overcooking or boiling.

## What are the Requirements for Canning at Home?

1. **Jar lifter Tongs**: Tongs aid in the safe removal of hot jars from hot water after the processing.
2. **Ladle**: To spoon food into the canning jars, use a ladle.
3. **Wide-mouth funnel**: A wide-mouth funnel has a bigger hole to accommodate jars. It makes filling your jars a lot easier and keeps the rims clean.
4. **Jars**
5. **Water-bath canner**: If you're primarily interested in fruits, jellies, jams, pickles, and salsa, a large pot or water-bath canner will suffice.

## What can be canned

- Fruits
- Tomatoes
- Vegetables
- Meat, poultry, and fish are all options.
- Jellies and jams
- Fermented veggies and pickles

# Chapter 3.
# Why Go Through the Effort of Canning?

To get the benefits of canning, you don't need a vast garden or a large-scale business. Even if your garden produces a few jars of your favorite vegetables, canning will reduce waste and preserve your crop, primarily if your garden produces more summer vegetables than you can consume right away.

It can help you save your money on groceries while also giving you a sense of pride and self-sufficiency in food storage. You also control the components, including additives and preservatives, because you can find your vegetables. It can be pretty beneficial for both mindful eating and unique dietary requirements. Regardless of why you choose to can, you must understand when and how to can summer vegetables properly.

## How to Prevent Darkening Food

Water or syrup should completely cover anything you're canning. Before closing the jars, be sure to remove any air bubbles and utilize the required headspace depending on the recipe.

## Floating Fluid

Do you have any jars with floating fruits in them? Fruits and tomatoes that have been over-processed might lose their natural pectin. Fruit may also float if the fruit is lighter weight than the sugar syrups or if it has been inappropriately packed.

**What to Do If Your Fruit Is Floating?**

It's a simple repair if you detect floating fruit. The essential thing is to follow the instructions for processing periods to prevent over-processing the delicate fruits. Before packaging the fruit, warm it up. Fruits, unlike vegetables, should not be packed uncooked. Use a light or medium syrup and compress the fruit carefully to prevent crushing it.

Canning, like gardening, is a skill that takes time to master. Making errors is an integral part of learning a new skill, so don't give up if you commit one of the most frequent canning blunders. Learn how to correct and avoid these blunders so that your canned foods endure for years in your cupboard.

# CHAPTER 4.
# WATER BATH CANNING

It's now time to fill your cupboard with jars of your prepared treats that the entire family will appreciate. This technique should never be attempted with non-acidic vegetables, soup, various stocks, meat, fish, or fowl. These need more complex methods, including the use of a pressure canner. These foods are not suitable for water bath canning.

## ADDITIONAL EQUIPMENT

The list above is technically all you need to get started. However, other tools can help to streamline the process.

The ever-popular Mason jars recently updated their instructions, noting that this step is no longer required when using them. However, many other manufacturers still need this first step in an old-fashioned manner, so double-check beforehand.

Before filling, all jars and lids must be cleansed with hot, soapy water, rinsed, and well dried. If this sounds too time-consuming, you might alternatively put the jars through a washing cycle. You'll need to work quickly to keep your canning jars and lids at the proper temperature following the washing.

# Topping Things Off

Then, using an actual clean, wet cloth, wipe any evidence of the food from the rims. The next step is to put the circular canning lids on the jars. If you can get your hands on a magnetic lid wand, you'll discover that it's a lifesaver. It enables you to rapidly and effectively grasp them one at a time. You'll want to screw them on as tightly as possible.

# Processing the Jars

The canning process starts by bringing a kettle of water to a full boil. During this time, your jars should be covered. The temperature can be adjusted, but you must maintain a gentle but thorough boil for the entire processing time. It is best to keep the water level one to two inches above the tops of the jars. If the water stops boiling during processing, you will need to restart the process.

When canning fruit, it is best to cook the fruit thoroughly. This will help to break down the cell walls and prevent the fruit from floating during the process. After cooking, allow the fruit to rest for 5 minutes before filling the jars. Do not process the jars for longer than the recipe directs. After the jars are sealed, you should carefully flip them over.

You can also sterilize jars by leaving them in boiling water for 10 minutes. This will help prevent the development of microorganisms, which may harm the foods you preserve. If you use a dishwasher, you can leave the jars in the machine until you are ready to use them. However, if you are processing your jars in a canner, you must keep them hot until the time is up. Otherwise, the food will become over-processed and lose all vitamins and minerals. If you aren't using the jars immediately, you can store them in a refrigerator for as long as you need to, but it's best to process them immediately after they have been sealed.

Once the jars have been processed, you should turn off the canner. If you have a jar lifter, you should remove them from the canner in a single motion, and place them on a towel or cake cooling rack. Make sure the jars are at least an inch apart. Make sure not to place the jars on a cold surface or in a draft, as this could lead to condensation.

After processing the jars, ensure the lids are securely on the jars. You may also want to check the labels of the processed jars. If the jars do not seal, they should be cleaned with hot soapy water. After this, you can heat the jars in the oven or water bath. When your jars have reached the desired temperature, you can store them in a root cellar or pantry. Water bath canners are great for preserving foods. The water bath canner should be tall enough to hold the jars. The water should also be hot enough to hold the jars in place. Depending on the size of the jars, you may need to use a jar lifter to lift the jars into the canner. Peaches are traditionally canned in sugar syrup, which is unnecessary for safe canning. Instead, try using a mixture of unsweetened fruit juice and water.

# The Cool Down

When the processing time for your water bath canning has ended, turn off the heat, let the jars find their equilibrium, and settle for about five minutes. Set the timer again to help you keep track.

Then, remove the jars from their rack using the tongs, lifting them vertically, and be very careful not to tilt them. They're at a vulnerable stage, so be careful with them. Otherwise, the food will touch the lid, something you do not want at this stage since you're still trying to make sure everything will be shelf-stable, with a perfect seal.

Transfer the jars to a cooling rack, or simply place many towels on the counter to protect your surfaces from the hot glass. Make sure to actually keep a distance of at least one inch between each jar. The towels or cooling rack is very important because you don't want the temperature of the jars to drop suddenly.

The temperature shock can cause them to break. Make sure that your jars are left without anyone shaking them or moving the contents around for at least twelve to fourteen hours until they've completely cooled. Any movement at this juncture will cause the lids to flex, which can break the seal, so keep them still.

Once in a while, the lid will make a small sound. This is the seal settling with the new temperature and is generally a good sign.

# CHAPTER 5.
## WATER BATH CANNING TIPS

D o your water-bath canning on an electric or gas stovetop. No matter what you've heard or how cool it sounds, it's not safe to can in an oven, microwave, or dishwasher. It's also not safe to can tomatoes and fruit products by simply sterilizing the jars and lids by boiling in water and then ladling a boiling-hot product into the jars, and sealing them by placing a lid and screw band on. Even if the jars seal well and hold their seal, their contents HAVE NOT been heated adequately to prevent bacteria, toxins, molds and yeast to grow when the jars are stored at room temperature.

Although some of the new multi-cookers come with a canning feature, the U.S. Department of Agriculture (USDA) says research warns that ALL of these devices are NOT SAFE for home canning, even for high-acid foods.

But the good news is that, even though pressure canning isn't nearly as scary as most people think, water bath canning is even less scary. In fact, it's downright safe and easy as long as you follow some very basic rules.

Smooth glass stovetops pose another concern for home canners. Some styles of water-bath canners have indented bottoms that prevent heat from the glass top from being adequately distributed during processing and much of the heat may be reflected from the canner back to the glass, causing the glass to overheat. This may cause the glass to crack, or activate the burner's shut-off feature, resulting in an under-processed canner-load.

If you have a smooth, glass cooking surface, the USDA says your best bet is to follow your stove manufacturer's advice, "because styles of smooth cooktops being manufactured differ in ways that influence suitability for canning."

# CHAPTER 6.
# WATER BATH CANNING EQUIPMENT

The thought of purchasing water bath canning equipment can seem quite daunting to most people. Still, the good news is that new-age kits have been designed especially for newbie home canners with racks made of silicon and with the provision of holding up to four jars at ago that can easily fit into your stock pot.

Having rubber tongs that you can use to pick up super-hot jars will come in real handy but not to worry if you don't have these as you can improvise with wrapping a cloth around your regular tongs. You are going to need:

- A six-quart metal pot
- An extra-large pot for the sterilization of jars and their lids
- Canning jars, rings, and lids
- Metal ladles
- Paper towels or dish cloths

- Metal funnel
- Tongs for grabbing jars

The jars should be clean and dry before you put in any food, and you should clean the jars at least three times before use.

A metallic funnel makes the canning process extra neat with no spillage on the sides of the jars. A metal funnel is suitable because it can withstand hot temperatures better than plastic funnels.

While most recipes call for a ¼ inch head space, it is advisable to leave 1 inch of space to expand the food content during the water bath process. However, the amount of headspace will also depend on the recipe you are preparing, but to be safe, leave an inch.

Once you have filled the jars, run a very thin, non-metal spatula inside your jars, gently pressing to remove any air bubbles. Once you have done this, use a clean and damp towel to wipe any food particles to allow for a tight seal.

Place the now softened lids onto the rims, gently screwing until they are tightly in place. If it's too hot to handle, wait until the jars have cooled enough to handle, then give it the tightest close

# WATER BATH PROCESSING

The first thing you need to do in this step is to ensure that the amount of water in your kettle is enough to fully cover the tops of the jars you are processing and bring the water to a rolling boil for 3 minutes. Meanwhile, place the jars into your rack, and once your water is ready, gently lower them into the kettle and cover it. For most recipes, you will need 10-15 minutes of processing but to be safe, be sure to follow the recipe instructions.

Once the processing time has elapsed, remove the cover from the kettle and use your tongs to remove your jars to a sterile and dry place and let them stand, undisturbed for a full hour.

Once the hour elapses after processing, you can wipe them completely dry, put appropriate labels including the date and move the jars to your pantry in a cool and dry place, away from sunlight, and admire your good job! Congratulations! This means you have enough food to take you through at least 9 months!

As we said earlier, if you are ready to eat on opening your jars, you realize that the jars don't seal when they bulge out or when the food becomes dark and produces a bad smell, discard your food.

Don't insist on eating such food as it could have harmful toxins. Just go through the process and try again; mistakes happen, but we don't let them stop us!

You will note that we have said that you can preserve food in the fridge in some recipes. However, you can use the canning process for all recipes in our book. All the ingredients allow for both canning and preservation in the refrigerator.

# Chapter 7.
# Canning and Preserving Safety Tips

## Food in Jars Extends the Life of Food

Food in jars extends the life cycle of food by eliminating the risk of spoilage caused by microorganisms. The heat from the canning process kills most of the bacteria that cause food to spoil, and the vacuum seal prevents outside air from entering the jar. A variety of different foods can be preserved in jars.

Many grocery stores have expanded their freezers to offer a wider variety of items for freezing. This has made it easier to find more varieties of food and has resulted in a longer lifespan for many types of items. But while it is true that storing food in jars can significantly increase the shelf life of food, there are also several risks involved. The first issue is that the vacuum sealing method does not completely remove all of the oxygen. In addition, it can trap some moisture from the food. In some cases, this moisture could support the growth of molds and bacteria.

# PREVENTS GROWTH OF UNDESIRABLE BACTERIA

Preventing the growth of undesirable bacteria while canning and preserving is important to keep food safe. Proper canning will remove oxygen and destroy enzymes, preventing the growth of bacteria that can cause harmful illnesses. It also prevents the formation of molds and yeasts. When done incorrectly, canning can result in botulism, a bacterial infection that can lead to death.

One way to prevent bacteria is to make sure the food is stored at the proper temperature. Bacteria grow best in a temperature between 40 and 140 degrees Fahrenheit. Using a pressure canner to seal the jars prevents these bacteria from growing. Proper canning also creates a vacuum that prevents the growth of harmful bacteria.

# ACIDITY IN HOME CANNED FOODS DETERMINES METHOD OF CANNING

The method used to can home canned foods depends on the acidity of the food. High acid foods are best processed in a water bath canner while low acid foods require pressure canning. The acid content may be natural or added. Low-acid canned foods do not have enough acid to prevent the growth of botulism, while high-acid foods degrade more quickly under high heat.

Foods whose pH value is lower than 4.6 are considered low-acid. To process these foods, add lemon juice or citric acid to the water before adding it to the canner. Those foods with pH values greater than 4.6 should use a pressure canner.

Salt does NOT play a preservative role in canning

Canning is the process of preserving foods in a water bath. The process is safe when the water is kept at a steady temperature. Salt plays a flavouring role. It is not used in large enough quantities to prevent spoilage. However, it is essential to use real salt when fermenting foods.

Canning without salt can be done by following traditional recipes or relying on reliable freezing and canning directions. However, be careful when substituting salt. Some salt substitutes have additives that can contribute to off flavors and colors. In addition, you may end up with cloudy brines.

## PRESSURE CANNING PREVENTS BOTULISM

Botulism is a foodborne disease that affects the stomach and is most common in seafood. Luckily, there are ways to prevent botulism in canned food. One of the best ways is to make sure the food is properly preserved. One way to prevent botulism is to can foods at a high enough pressure to destroy the bacteria. The pressure should be high enough for the type of food being canned, but not so high that it becomes too hot.

Botulism is caused by a bacterium called Clostridium botulinum. This organism can survive in water and soil for years, but it needs the right conditions to grow. This bacterium then produces the botulinum toxin, which causes death and paralysis in humans. In order to prevent botulism, you should always use modern canning techniques, according to the CDC.

## CHOOSE THE RIGHT CANNER

The first step to safe home canning is choosing the right canner.

If your canner has a rubber gasket, it should be flexible and soft. If the rubber is dry or cracked, it should be replaced before you start canning.

## OPT FOR A SCREW TOP LID SYSTEM

There are many kinds of canning jars that you can choose to purchase. However, the only type of jar approved by the USDA is a Mason jar with a screw-top lid. These are designated "preserving jars" and are considered the safest and most effective option for home preserving uses.

Some jars are not thought to be safe for home preservation despite being marketed as canning jars. Bail Jars, for example, have a two-part wire clasp lid with a rubber ring in between the lid and jar. While these were popular in the past, it is now thought that the thick rubber and tightly closed lid do not provide a sufficient seal, leading to a higher potential for botulism. Lightening Jars should not be used for canning as they are simply glass jars with glass lids, with no rubber at all. That will not create a good seal!

Reusing jars from store-bought products is another poor idea. They may look like they're in good condition, but they are typically designed to be processed in a commercial facility. Most store-bought products do not have the two-part band and lid system, best for home canning. Also, the rubber seal on a store-bought product is likely not reusable once you open the original jar. You can reuse store-bought jars at home for storage but not for canning and preserving.

## Check Your Jars, Lids, and Bands

As you wash your jars with soapy water, check for any imperfections. Even new jars may have a small chip or crack and need to be discarded. You can reuse jars again and again as long as they are in good condition.

The metal jar rings are also reusable; however, you should only reuse them rust-free and undented. If your bands begin to show signs of wear, consider investing in some new ones.

## Check for Recent Canning Updates

Many people used to sterilize their jars before pressure canning. While this is still okay, it is not necessary, as science has shown that any bacteria in the jars will die when heated to such a high temperature in a pressure canner. Sterilization is an extra step that you just don't need!

Make sure that your food preservation information is all up to date and uses current canning guidelines.

## Pick the Best Ingredients

When choosing food to can, always get the best food possible. You want to use high-quality, perfectly ripe produce for canning. You will never end up with a jar of food better than the product itself, so picking good ingredients is important to the taste of your final product. If strawberries are overripe, your jam may come out too runny. Pick your ingredients well, and you will make successfully preserved foods.

# Clean Everything

While you may know that your jars and lids need to be washed and sanitized, don't forget about the rest of your tools. Cleaning out your canner before using it is essential, even if you put it away clean. Make sure to wipe your countertop well, making sure there are no crumbs or residue. Wash your produce with clean, cold water, and don't forget to wash your hands! The cleaner everything is, the less likely you are to spread bacteria onto your jarred foods.

# Follow Your Recipe

Use recipes from trusted sources and be sure to follow them to the letter. Changing the amount of one or two ingredients may alter the balance of acidity and result in unsafe canning (especially when using a water bath canner). Use the ingredients as directed and make very few changes - if possible.

# Cool the Jars

Be sure that you give your jars 12 hours to cool before testing the seal. Testing the seal too early may break as the jar is still warm, making the rubber pliable. Once cool, remove the metal band, clean it and save it for your next canning project.

# Don't Risk it

Each time you open a jar of canned food, inspect it and check for the following:

1. Is the lid bulging, swollen, or leaking at all?
2. Is the jar cracked or damaged?
3. Does the jar foam when opened?
4. Is the food inside discolored or moldy?
5. Does the food smell bad?

A dent in the lid, a small crack in the jar, an improper seal, or insufficient processing time are all common errors that may cause canned foods to go bad. Follow the exact canning directions, and hopefully, you will never get a bad jar of food!

# Chapter 8.
# Jam Recipes

## 1. Blueberry Vanilla Jam

**Serving Size: 22 half-pint jars**

**Preparation Time: 15 minutes**

**Cooking Time: 22 minutes**

**Ingredients:**

- 6 large canning bottles
- 1 ¼ pounds of blueberries, rinsed and stems removed
- ¾ cup of granulated sugar
- 2 tablespoons of lemon juice

- ½ vanilla bean pod, seeds scraped
- 1 teaspoon of pectin

**Directions:**

1. Sterilize the bottles in a water bath canner. Allow the bottles to cool.
2. Place all ingredients except for the pectin in a pot and mash until the blueberries are macerated.
3. Set on the heat and bring to a boil for 10 minutes while stirring constantly. Remove the vanilla bean pod and stir in the pectin. Continue stirring for another 2 minutes until the mixture becomes thick.
4. Ladle into the sterilized jars and leave ¼ inch of headspace. Remove the air bubbles and screw the lid on.
5. Place in a water bath canner and follow the general instructions for water bath canning.
6. Process for 10 minutes.
7. Consume within a year and keep refrigerated once the bottles are opened.

# 2. Carrot Pineapple Jam

**Serving Size: 8 half-pints**

**Preparation Time: 45 minutes**

**Cooking Time: 5 minutes**

**Ingredients:**

- 20 ounces of crushed pineapple, undrained
- 1 ½ cups of peeled, shredded carrots
- 1 ½ cups of ripe, peeled, chopped pears
- 3 tablespoons of lemon juice
- 1 teaspoon of ground cinnamon
- ¼ teaspoon of ground cloves
- ¼ teaspoon of ground nutmeg
- 1 package of powdered fruit pectin
- 6 ½ cups of sugar

**Directions:**

1. In a medium saucepan, bring the first 7 ingredients to a boil.
2. Reduce heat to low and cook, covered, for 15-20 minutes, or until pears are cooked, stirring occasionally.
3. Add pectin. Bring to a full boil, stirring constantly.
4. Stir in sugar. Boil and stir for 1 minute.
5. Remove from heat and skim off foam.
6. Scoop the heated mixture into half-pint jars that have been sterilized, leaving a 14-inch gap at the top. Remove any air bubbles and, if necessary, correct headspace with hot mix. Wipe the rims with a soft cloth. Screw on bands until fingertip tight. Place caps on jars and screw on bands until fingertip tight.
7. Fill the canner halfway with hot water, making sure the jars are completely submerged. Allow 10 minutes for the water to boil. Remove the jars and set them aside to cool.

# 3. Green Tomato Jam

**Serving Size: 3 half-pints**

**Preparation Time: 10 minutes**

**Cooking Time: 20 minutes**

**Ingredients:**

- 2 ½ cups of pureed green tomatoes
- 2 cups of sugar
- 1 package of raspberry gelatin

**Directions:**

1. Bring the sugar and tomatoes to a boil in a large saucepan.
2. Reduce heat to low and cook for 20 minutes, uncovered.
3. Remove the pan from the heat and stir in the gelatin until it dissolves completely.
4. Skim off any foam.
5. Scoop the heated mixture into half-pint sterilized jars, leaving a 14-inch gap at the top.
6. Remove any air bubbles and, if necessary, correct headspace with hot mix. Wipe the rims with a soft cloth. Allow cooling completely before covering with lids. Keep refrigerated for up to three weeks.

# 4. Maple Blackberry Jam

**Serving Size: 6 half-pint jars**

**Preparation Time: 15 minutes**

**Cooking Time: 1 hour**

**Ingredients:**

- 6 canning bottles
- 6 cups of blackberries, crushed
- 1 ½cup of pure maple syrup
- Zest and juice from one lemon

**Directions:**

1. Sterilize the bottles in a water bath canner. Allow the bottles to cool.
2. Set all ingredients in a saucepan and bring to a simmer. Cook for 50 minutes while constantly stirring over medium-low heat or until the mixture thickens.
3. Dip an old spoon into the jam and tip gently. The jam is ready if it runs off in a sheet and the liquid does not drip.
4. Set off the heat and allow the mixture to cool slightly before transferring into the sterilized bottles.
5. Remove the air bubbles in the mixture. Close the lid and place it in the water bath canner.
6. Process for 10 minutes.
7. Store in a cool dark place and consume within a year.

# 5. MULBERRY JAM

**Serving Size: 14**

**Preparation Time: 15 minutes**

**Cooking Time: 30 minutes**

**Ingredients:**

- 6 cups of mulberries
- 2 cups of plus 1 tablespoon of water, divided
- ¾ cup of white sugar
- 1 (3-ounces) package strawberry-flavored gelatin
- 1 (1 ¾-ounces) package powdered fruit pectin

**Directions:**

1. In a large stainless-steel saucepan, place mulberries and 1 tbsp. of water and bring to a boil.
2. Now set the heat to low and cook, covered for about 15-20 minutes, stirring frequently.
3. Meanwhile, in a non-reactive bowl, add remaining water, sugar, gelatin and pectin and stir until gelatin is dissolved.
4. With a potato masher, mash the berries.
5. Stir in the sugar mixture and bring to a boil.
6. In 8 (½-pint) hot sterilized jars, divide the berry mixture, leaving about ½-inch space from the top.
7. Slide a small knife around the insides of each jar to remove air bubbles.
8. Wipe any trace of food off the rims of jars with a clean, moist kitchen towel.
9. Close each jar with a lid and screw on the ring.
10. Arrange the jars in a boiling water canner and process for about 10 minutes.
11. Remove the jars from water canner and place onto a wood surface several inches apart to cool completely.
12. After cooling with your finger, press the top of each jar's lid to ensure that the seal is tight.
13. The canned jam can be stored in the pantry for up to 1 year.

# Chapter 9.
# Jelly Recipes

## 6. Apple Cinnamon Jelly

**Serving Size: 7 half-pints**

**Preparation Time: 10 minutes**

**Cooking Time: 30 minutes**

**Ingredients:**

- 4 cups of unsweetened apple juice
- 1 package of powdered fruit pectin
- 6 ½ cups of sugar
- 2 teaspoons of ground cinnamon

- ¼ teaspoon of ground cloves
- ¼ teaspoon of fresh ground nutmeg

**Directions:**

1. Mix pectin and apple juice in a Dutch oven. Bring the mixture to a full rolling boil on high heat while stirring continuously. Mix the remaining ingredients in a bowl, then stir into the apple mixture and bring back to a full rolling boil. Boil and stir for 3 minutes.
2. Take away from the heat and skim off foam. Scoop hot mixture carefully into 7 hot sterilized ½-pint jars, leaving ¼ inch headspace. Wipe the rims, put the lid on the center of jars, and screw on bands until fingertip tight.
3. Put jars into canner with simmering water, making sure to cover jars completely with water. Bring to a boil and process for 5 minutes. Take jars out of the water and allow cooling.

# 7. CRANBERRY AND ORANGE JELLY

**Serving Size: 4 pints**

**Preparation Time: 15 minutes**

**Cooking Time: 20 minutes**

**Ingredients:**

- 1 pound of fresh cranberries
- 5 to 10 whole cloves
- 1 whole star anise
- Juice & zest of 2 oranges
- 1 to 1 ½ cups water (depending on how juicy the cranberries are)
- ¾ to 1 cup white (granulated) sugar (to taste)
- ¼ teaspoon ground allspice
- ¼ teaspoon ground cinnamon
- Pinch of salt

**Directions:**

1. Put all the ingredients into a saucepan, ensuring the cranberries are covered with water
2. Bring to the boil, cover, reduce the heat and simmer for about 10 minutes (you should hear the cranberries popping during this time)
3. Reduce the heat and taste - stirring in the sugar to get your desired sweetness. Cook for another 5 or 10 minutes to thicken
4. Test setting point but note it will thicken considerably on cooling. Serve warm, or jar refrigerate and eat later

## 8. ELDERBERRY JELLY

**Serving Size: 5**

**Preparation Time: 10 minutes**

**Cooking Time: 35 minutes**

**Ingredients:**

- 4 pounds of crushed elderberries
- 1 packet of pectin
- ¼ cup of lemon juice
- ¼ teaspoon of butter
- 4 ½ cups of sugar

**Directions:**

1. Add the crushed elderberries into a pot.
2. Place the pot on the stove over medium heat. Bring the elderberries to a boil while continuing to crush them.
3. Simmer for 10 minutes before removing the pot from the stove.
4. Strain the mixture through a sieve held over a clean pot. You want the juice of the berries to go into the pot.
5. Add the pectin following the instructions on the packet. Stir in the lemon juice.
6. Boil and stir in the butter and sugar. Continue constantly stirring until the jelly reaches a rolling boil. Continue to boil for 2 minutes.
7. Pour the jelly into the jars, leaving about ¼ an inch of space in each jar. Attach the lids.
8. Process the jars using the water bath canning method for 5 to 10 minutes.

# 9. GRAPE JELLY

**Serving Size: 3 pints**

**Preparation Time: 10 minutes**

**Cooking Time: 20 minutes**

**Ingredients:**

- 2 tablespoons gelatin powder
- 2 tablespoons lemon juice
- 24 ounces of grape juice
- 2 tablespoons artificial sweetener

**Directions:**

1. Mix gelatin with lemon juice and grape juice in a saucepan to soften it, then bring to a hard boil. Let boil for approximately about 1 minute then remove from heat. Add the actual sweetener and stir until well combined.
2. Pour the hot liquid in sterilized pint jars leaving a ¼-inch headspace. Use a clean damp cloth to actually wipe the jar rims and put on the lids.
3. Place the jars in the pressure canner with water such that the jars are covered by water at least 2-inches.
4. Cover the pressure canner with an ordinary lid that fits well and process the pint jars for 10 minutes in the boiling water. Remove the prepared jars from the canner and cool overnight.

# 10. Lime Mint Jelly

**Serving Size: 5 half-pints**

**Preparation Time: 10 minutes**

**Cooking Time: 10 minutes**

**Ingredients:**

- 4 cups of sugar
- 1 ¾ cups of water
- ¾ cup of lime juice
- 3 drops of green food coloring
- 1 package of liquid fruit pectin
- 3 tablespoons of chopped fresh mint leaves
- ¼ cup of grated lime zest

**Directions:**

1. Combine lime juice, sugar, water, and food coloring in a big pot. Bring to a rolling boil, continually stirring.
2. Stir in lime zest pectin and mint. Continue boiling for 1 minute, stirring constantly.
3. Remove from heat and skim off foam.
4. Scoop the heated mixture into half-pint jars that have been sterilized, leaving a 14-inch gap at the top. Remove any air bubbles and, if necessary, correct headspace with hot mix. Wipe the rims with a soft cloth. Screw on bands until fingertip tight. Place caps on jars and screw on bands until fingertip tight.
5. Fill the canner halfway with hot water, making sure the jars are thoroughly submerged. Allow 10 minutes for the water to come to a rolling boil. Remove the jars and set them aside to cool.

# Chapter 10.
# Chutney Recipes

## 11. Cantaloupe Chutney

**Serving Size: 3 pints**

**Preparation Time: 15 minutes**

**Cooking Time: 1 hour 30 minutes**

**Ingredients:**

- 3 medium cantaloupes
- 1 pound of dried apricots
- 1 fresh hot chili
- 2 cups of raisins

- 1 teaspoon of ground cloves
- 1 teaspoon of ground nutmeg
- 2 tablespoons of salt
- 2 tablespoons of mustard seed
- ¼ cup fresh ginger, chopped
- 3 cloves garlic
- 4 ½ cups apple cider vinegar
- 2 ¼ cups brown sugar
- 4 onions
- ½ cup orange juice
- 2 tablespoons of orange zest

**Directions:**

1. Thinly slice the apricots and put them into a large bowl.
2. Chop the ginger and garlic thinly, and add to the dish.
3. Stir in chili, seed, and dice, and add to the pot.
4. Add raisins, cloves, cinnamon, nutmeg, and mustard seeds.
5. Mix together and set aside.
6. Combine the vinegar and sugar in a non-reactive pot or kettle; bring to a boil over medium heat.
7. Add mixture to the pot in a bowl and return to a moderate simmer.
8. Keep simmer for 45 minutes. Do not deck the pot.
9. Meanwhile, onions are chopped and placed in a bowl.
10. Cantaloupes fifth, peel, and seed.
11. Split the fruit into half-inch cubes.
12. Add onions.
13. In cup, add orange juice and zest; mix well.
14. Once the vinegar mixture has ended 45 minutes of cooking time, add the cantaloupe mixture to the bowl, bring it back to a cooler, and start cooking for another 45 minutes or until thickened at the simmer.
15. Pour into hot glasses, clean the rims, screw the lids and rings together.
16. Boiling water bath process: pints and quarts 10 minutes in, both.

# 12. Garlicky Lime Chutney

**Serving Size: 2**

**Preparation Time: 25 minutes**

**Cooking Time: 1 hour**

**Ingredients:**

- 12 diced limes
- 12 sliced garlic cloves
- 1 sliced ginger
- 8 green chile peppers
- 1 tablespoon of chili powder
- 1 cup of distilled white vinegar
- ¾ cup of sugar

**Directions:**

1. Prepare a hot water bath. Place the jars in it to keep warm. Wash the lids and rings in hot, soapy water, and set them aside.
2. In a medium saucepan, combine the limes, garlic, ginger, chiles, and chili powder. Stir well, and bring to a simmer.
3. Stir in the sugar and vinegar, then simmer for 1 hour 10 minutes
4. Ladle the chutney into the prepared jars, leaving ¼ inch of headspace.
5. Rinse the rims clean and seal with the lids and rings.
6. Process the jars in a hot water bath for 20 minutes.

205

# 13. Orange Cranberry Chutney

**Serving Size: 3-pint jars**

**Preparation Time: 15 minutes**

**Cooking Time: 20 minutes**

**Ingredients:**

- 2 cups of chopped white onion
- 2 cups of white vinegar
- 3 cinnamon sticks
- 1¾ cups of sugar
- 4 tablespoons of grated ginger
- 24 ounces of fresh cranberries
- 2 cups of golden raisins
- 1 cup of orange juice

**Directions:**

1. After thoroughly rinsing the cranberries, put them in a Dutch oven (large).
2. Add other ingredients and toss to combine.
3. Boil the mixture over high heat.
4. Simmer for 15 minutes or until you're sure the cranberries are tenderized. Make sure to stir to avoid scorching frequently.
5. Once the chutney is done, discard the cinnamon sticks. Pour the chutney into clean and hot Mason jars (half-pint), making sure to leave half an inch of headspace in each.
6. Get rid of air bubbles in the jars before fitting their rims with the lids. Place in the pressure canner.
7. Process for 10 minutes.

# 14. Raisin Pear Chutney

**Serving Size: 2-pint jars**

**Preparation Time: 15 minutes**

**Cooking Time: 20 minutes**

**Ingredients:**

- 2 cups of cider vinegar
- 1¼ cups of packed brown sugar
- 3 pounds of unpeeled ripe pears, diced
- 1 chopped onion
- 1 cup of raisins
- 2 teaspoons of ground cinnamon
- 1 teaspoon of ground cloves
- 1 minced garlic clove
- 1 teaspoon of cayenne pepper

**Directions:**

1. In a saucepan, bring brown sugar and vinegar to a boil.
2. Stir in the remaining ingredients and return to a boil.
3. Reduce heat and let simmer uncovered for 2 hours to 2 hours 15 minutes until chutney reaches desired consistency.
4. Carefully scoop hot mixture into hot sterilized pint jars, leaving ¼ -inch headspace. Remove any air bubbles and adjust headspace as needed by adding an extra heated mixture. Wipe the rims with a soft cloth. Screw on bands until fingertip tight. Place caps on jars and screw on bands until fingertip tight.
5. Fill the canner halfway with hot water, making sure the jars are thoroughly submerged. Let boil for 15 minutes. Remove jars and cool.

# 15. Rhubarb Cherry Chutney

**Serving Size: 6 cups**

**Preparation Time: 20 minutes**

**Cooking Time: 35 minutes**

**Ingredients:**

- 2 pounds of chopped fresh rhubarb
- 2 cups of fresh pitted tart cherries, chopped
- 1 large tart apple, peeled, chopped
- 1 medium red onion, chopped
- 1 celery rib, chopped
- 3 garlic cloves, minced
- 1 tablespoon of finely chopped crystallized ginger
- 2 cups of brown sugar
- 1 cup of red wine vinegar
- ¾ teaspoon of ground cinnamon
- ½ teaspoon of ground coriander
- ¼ teaspoon of ground cloves

**Directions:**

1. In a 6-quart stockpot, combine all ingredients. Bring to boil.
2. Reduce heat, then simmer, uncovered, 25-30 minutes, until thickened.
3. Transfer to covered containers. If freezing, use freezer-safe containers and fill to within ½ inch of tops. Freeze up to 12 months or refrigerate up to 3 weeks. Before serving, thaw frozen salsa in the refrigerator.

# Chapter II.
# Marmalade Recipes

## 16. Clementine Marmalade

**Serving Size: 10**

**Preparation Time: 15 minutes**

**Cooking Time: 16 minutes**

**Ingredients:**

- ½ lemon
- 8 whole clementines
- 2 cups of water
- 3 ½ cups of white sugar

**Directions:**

1. Squeeze the lemon halves, reserving the juice in a cup.
2. In a cheesecloth, tie the lemon seeds.
3. In a non-reactive saucepan, add clementines, water, squeezed lemon halves and the bundle of lemon seeds over medium-high heat and simmer, covered for about 2-3 hours.
4. Remove the saucepan of clementine mixture from the heat and set aside overnight.
5. Discard the bundle of lemon seeds.
6. With a prepared slotted spoon, remove the fruit from liquid and transfer into a bowl.
7. Cut the clementines in half and scoop pulp and seeds.
8. Through a strainer, strain the pulp in the same pan by pressing with the back of a spoon.
9. Reserve all peels.
10. In the pan, add the sugar and lemon juice over medium-low heat and cook for about 2-3 minutes, stirring continuously.
11. Meanwhile, cut the clementine peel into fine very thin slices.
12. In the pan, add the peel slices and cook for about 5-10 minutes, stirring occasionally.
13. In ⅕ PINT hot sterilized jars, divide the marmalade, leaving about ½-inch space from the top.
14. Slide a small knife around the insides of each jar to remove air bubbles.
15. Wipe any trace of food off the rims of jars with a clean, moist kitchen towel.
16. Close each jar with a lid and screw on the ring.
17. Arrange the jars in a boiling water canner and process for about 10 minutes.
18. Remove the jars from water canner and place onto a wood surface several inches apart to cool completely.
19. After cooling with your finger, press the top of each jar's lid to ensure that the seal is tight.
20. The canned marmalade can be stored in the pantry for up to 1 year.

# 17. Lemon Marmalade

**Serving Size: 6 half-pints**

**Preparation Time: 40 minutes**

**Cooking Time: 10 minutes**

**Ingredients:**

- 3 medium lemons
- 1 medium grapefruit
- 4 cups of water
- 1 package of powdered fruit pectin
- 4 cups of sugar

**Directions:**

1. Peel rind from lemons and grapefruit, cut into 1-inch long strips.
2. In a Dutch oven, combine citrus peel and water. Bring to boil. Reduce heat, then simmer, covered, 5-7 minutes, until peel softened. Remove from heat, then set it aside.
3. Trim the white pith from reserved grapefruit and lemons. Cut grapefruit and lemons in segments, discarding seeds and membranes.
4. Chop pulp, reserving juices, and then stir into reserved peel mixture.
5. Add pectin. Bring to boil, stirring constantly.
6. Stir in sugar while letting it boil, stirring, 1 minute.
7. Remove from heat and skim off foam.
8. Scoop hot mixture into 6 hot sterilized half-pint jars, leave ¼-inch headspace. Remove the air bubbles and, if necessary, adjust headspace by adding a hot mixture. Wipe rims carefully. Place the tops on jars and screw on bands until fingertip tight.
9. Place jars in a canner with boiling water, ensuring they are completely covered with water. Let boil for 10 minutes. Remove jars and cool.

# 18. Orange Marmalade

**Serving Size: 2-pint jars**

**Preparation Time: 15 minutes**

**Cooking Time: 15 minutes**

**Ingredients:**

- ½ cup of water
- 4 medium navel oranges, peeled and cut into small pieces
- 2 cups of sugar

**Directions:**

1. Add the orange pieces to a blender or food processor. Blend well.
2. In a deep saucepan, combine the orange mixture, water, and sugar.
3. Set the mixture till the thermometer reads 220°F; cook for about 12–15 minutes over medium heat until firm and thick. Stir continually to prevent scorching.
4. Spill the hot mixture into pre-sterilized jars directly or with a jar funnel. Keep headspace of ¼ inch from the jar top.
5. To detach tiny air bubbles, insert a nonmetallic spatula and stir the mixture gently.
6. Clean the sealing edges with a damp cloth. Secure the jars with the lids and adjust the bands/rings to seal and prevent any leakage.
7. Set the jars in a cool, dry, and dark place. Allow them to cool down completely.
8. Store in your refrigerator and use within 10 days.

# 19. Pineapple Marmalade

**Serving Size: 8-pint jars**

**Preparation Time: 10 minutes**

**Cooking Time: 45 minutes**

**Ingredients:**

- 3 ½ cups of shredded pineapple flesh
- ½ lemon, sliced
- 4 ½ cups of sugar
- 4 cups of water

**Directions:**

1. Add pineapple, lemon, and water to a saucepan. Cover and let sit overnight.
2. Boil pineapple mixture for 20 minutes.
3. Attach sugar and stir until sugar is dissolved.
4. Boil pineapple mixture for 25 minutes.
5. Remove saucepan from heat.
6. Pour the marmalade into the clean jars.
7. Seal jar with lids. Name and store in a cool and dry place.

# 20. Rhubarb Raisin Marmalade

**Serving Size: 4-pint jars**

**Preparation Time: 25 minutes**

**Cooking Time: 10 minutes**

**Ingredients:**

- 2 medium oranges
- 1 medium lemon
- 6 cups of sugar
- 6 cups of diced fresh or frozen rhubarb
- 1½ cups of fresh or frozen strawberries
- Pinch salt
- 1 cup of raisins

**Directions:**

1. Finely grate the skins of the oranges and lemons; squeeze the juices and set aside. Place the peels, juices, sugar, rhubarb, strawberries, and salt in a Dutch oven and mix well. Cook until sugar is melted, stirring frequently; mix in the raisins. Bring to a full rolling boil, then reduce to low heat and simmer for 5 minutes, or until the sauce has thickened. Remove the heat from the saucepan and skim out foam that has formed.
2. Ladle heated mixture into hot pint jars with care, allowing a 14-inch headspace. Air bubbles should be removed, rims should be cleaned, and lids should be adjusted. In a boiling water canner, the process is for 10 minutes.

# Chapter 12.
# Pickle Recipes

## 21. Bread and Butter Pickles

**Serving Size: 3 pints**

**Preparation Time: 30 minutes**

**Cooking Time: 20 minutes**

**Ingredients:**

- 15 cups of sliced pickling cucumbers
- 3 onions sliced thinly
- ¼ cup of salt
- 1 tablespoon of mustard seeds

- 2 ½ cups of cider vinegar
- 2 ½ cups of sugar
- ¾ teaspoon of turmeric
- ½ teaspoon of celery seed
- 6 cups of water

**Directions:**

1. Mix the onions, ice, salt, and cucumbers in a bowl.
2. Place a gallon of water or something heavy on the bowl and cover it with a plate. This acts as a counterweight. Allow it to sit for three hours.
3. After three hours, drain and rinse.
4. Combine the sugar, vinegar, celery seed, mustard seed, and turmeric in a large saucepan.
5. Add the cucumbers that have been drained.
6. In a medium-sized saucepan, bring the 6 cups of water nearly to a boil.
7. Remove from fire as soon as it reaches a boil and pour into sterilized jars.
8. Soak for 10 minutes in a hot water bath.
9. Dry them off and bake them for 15 minutes at 225°F on a baking sheet, right side up. This is done to guarantee no air pockets, that everything has been correctly cooked, and that everything has been disinfected and sealed before being kept. Before storage, let it cool fully.

# 22. Cherry Tomatoes Pickles

**Serving Size: 7 half-pint jars**

**Preparation Time: 30 minutes**

**Cooking Time: 15 minutes**

**Ingredients:**

- 4 ½ cups of water
- 4 cups of vinegar
- 1 cup of sugar
- 6 tablespoons of canning salt
- 8 cups of cherry tomatoes
- 2 cups of coarsely chopped celery
- 4 cups of coarsely chopped onion
- 2 cups of coarsely chopped sweet pepper
- 1 cup of cucamelon (optional)
- 6-7 garlic cloves
- 6-7 heads of dill

**Directions:**

1. Merge water, vinegar, salt, and sugar in a saucepot, large, and then boil.
2. Pack the vegetables to your hot jars and leave ¼-inch headspace. To each jar, attach 1 garlic clove and 1 head of dill.
3. Scoop hot liquid into the hot jars and leave ¼-inch headspace.
4. Now remove air bubbles checking headspace.
5. Clean jar rims with a clean cloth and applies 2-piece caps.
6. Process in a pressure canner for about 15 minutes following the manufacturer's guide and according to the altitude.

# 23. MUSHROOM PICKLES

**Serving Size: 30**

**Preparation Time: 5 minutes**

**Cooking Time: 15 minutes**

**Ingredients:**

- 5 pounds of small mushrooms
- 2 cups of white vinegar
- 1 ½ cups of canola oil
- 2 onions (halved, sliced)
- 2 tablespoons of canning salt
- ¼ teaspoon of dried tarragon
- 3 garlic cloves (minced)
- ¼ cup of sugar
- ½ teaspoon of pepper

**Directions:**

1. Sterilize the jars.
2. In a saucepan, combine all of the ingredients and bring to a boil.
3. Simmer for 10 minutes on low heat.
4. Carefully ladle the heated mixture into the sterilized jars, allowing a half-inch headspace.
5. Clean the rims and remove any air bubbles.
6. Place the lids on the jars and attach the bands, ensuring sure they are tight.
7. Process the jars for 20 minutes in a hot water canner that has been prepared.
8. Remove the jars from the oven, set them aside to cool, and then label them.

# 24. Sweet Pepper Pickles

**Serving Size: 24**

**Preparation Time: 15 minutes**

**Cooking Time: 20 minutes**

**Ingredients:**

- 5 sweet red peppers
- 1 onion
- 8 banana peppers
- 4 teaspoons of canola oil
- 1 ¼ cups of sugar
- 2 teaspoons of canning salt
- 8 garlic cloves
- 2 ½ cups of water
- 2 ½ cups of white vinegar

**Directions:**

1. Fill the jars with red peppers, banana peppers, garlic, onion, and oil after sterilizing them.
2. Bring the sugar, vinegar, salt, and water to a boil in a saucepan.
3. Carefully ladle the heated mixture into the sterilized jars, allowing a half-inch headspace.
4. Clean the rims and remove any air bubbles.
5. Place the lids on the jars and attach the bands, ensuring sure they are tight.
6. Process the jars for 15 minutes in a hot water canner that has been prepared.
7. Remove the jars from the oven, set them aside to cool, and then label them.

## 25. WATERMELON PICKLES

**Serving Size: 4 pints**

**Preparation Time: 30 minutes**

**Cooking Time: 10 minutes**

**Ingredients:**

- 2 pounds of watermelon rind
- 4 cups of sugar
- 2 cups of white vinegar
- 2 cups of water
- 1 sliced lemon
- 1 cinnamon stick
- 1 tablespoon of whole cloves

**Directions:**

1. Trim dark green and pink flesh from rind; cut into 1-inch cubes.
2. Combine ¼ pickling salt and 1 quart of water.
3. Heat and stir until salt is dissolved.
4. Pour saltwater over rind cubes. Leave overnight.
5. Drain and rinse cubes.
6. Place in heavy pot or kettle.
7. Cover with cold water and cook until tender; drain.
8. Combine sugar, vinegar, water, and lemon slices in a heavy pot.
9. Put the cinnamon and cloves in a cheesecloth bag and put the bag in the vinegar mixture.
10. Simmer the mixture for 10 minutes and remove the spice bag.
11. Add rind cubes to the vinegar mixture and continue cooking until cubes are translucent.
12. Pour into hot, sterile, pint jars, dividing syrup evenly and leaving ½-inch headspace.
13. Can jars in a boiling water bath for 15 minutes.

# Chapter 13.
# Relish Recipes

## 26. Apple Relish

**Serving Size: 4 pints**

**Preparation Time: 15 minutes**

**Cooking Time: 20 minutes**

**Ingredients:**

- 4 pounds of apples
- 3 quarts of water
- 1 ¼ cups of white vinegar, divided
- 1 cup of sugar

- ½ cup of light corn syrup
- ⅔ cup of water
- 2 teaspoons of whole cloves
- 1 ½ sticks of cinnamon

**Directions:**

1. Wash, pare, core, then cut apples into eighths. Place in a bowl containing 3 quarts of water and 4 tablespoons of vinegar to prevent darkening.
2. Combine sugar, corn syrup, rest of vinegar, ⅔ cup water, cloves, and cinnamon, broken into pieces, in a pot. Heat to boiling. Drain apples and add to the pot. Cover and boil for 3 minutes, stirring occasionally. Ladle hot relish in hot, sterilized jars, leave ¼ inch of headspace, filling with syrup, leaving ¼ inch of headspace. Wipe the jar's rim, set a warm lid in place, and tighten. Place in a bath canner with boiling water and process for 10 minutes.

# 27. Cucumber Relish

**Serving Size: 5 pints**

**Preparation Time: 45 minutes**

**Cooking Time: 25 minutes**

**Ingredients:**

- 4 unpeeled and diced cucumbers
- 2 diced green peppers
- 1 diced red pepper
- 1 tablespoon of celery seed
- 3 cups of ground onions
- 3 cups of finely diced celery
- ¼ cup of salt
- 2 cups of white vinegar
- 1 tablespoon of mustard seeds
- 3 ½ cups of sugar

**Directions:**

1. Place all ingredients in a food processor, then pulse until the cucumber is finely chopped.
2. Place the relish in a large bowl and cover with cold water, letting it sit for about 4 hours.
3. Drain the mixture and combine with sugar. Bring to a boil. As it heats up, liquids will come out. Stir until the sugar is dissolved.
4. Pack into jars, and let sit in the bath for about 10 minutes.
5. Let cool completely before storing.

## 23. Jalapeno Pepper Relish

**Serving Size: 8-pint jars**

**Preparation Time: 14 minutes**

**Cooking Time: 5 minutes**

**Ingredients:**

- 5 pounds of finely chopped jalapeño peppers
- 2 cups of sugar
- 4 cups of white vinegar
- ½ cup of cilantro leaves (optional)

**Directions:**

1. In a food processor, finely slice the peppers. Don't turn them into pureed mush; make them the consistency of a relish.
2. In a large pot, stir the sugar into the vinegar and bring it to a boil. Immediately turn off the heat once the boil is achieved.
3. Use your food processor to slice the cilantro leaves; if you are using them, stir them into your chopped peppers.
4. Ladle the uncooked peppers and cilantro into your canning jars, then spoon the liquid over the mixture, allowing ½ inch of headspace.
5. Set the jars in a water bath canner for 10 minutes, adjusting for altitude.

# 29. PEPPER RELISH

**Serving Size: 1-pint jar**

**Preparation Time: 20 minutes**

**Cooking Time: 10 minutes**

**Ingredients:**

- 2 tablespoons of green chilies, chopped
- ¼ cup each green, red, yellow pepper, chopped
- 1 tablespoon of jalapeno pepper
- 3 tablespoons of chopped onions, finely chopped
- ½ cup of water
- ½ tablespoon of salt
- 1 small bay leaf
- 1/8 tablespoon of coriander
- ¼ tablespoon of allspice, ground
- 3 tablespoons of white vinegar
- 2 tablespoons of sugar

**Directions:**

1. Place the chilies, peppers, and onions in a glass container.
2. Bring water and salt to boil in a saucepan, then pour the salted hot water over the pepper mixture.
3. Stir in the bay leaf. Coriander and allspice and refrigerate overnight.
4. Bring vinegar and sugar to boil, then reduce heat and simmer for 4 minutes or until all sugar has dissolved.
5. Drain the pepper mixture discarding the bay leaves, and transfer the mixture in sterilized hot pint jars. Pour over the vinegar mixture.
6. Process the jars in hot water in the pressure canner for 10 minutes.
7. Let the jars cool before labeling and storing them.

# 30. Zucchini Relish

**Serving Size: 16**

**Preparation Time: 15 minutes**

**Cooking Time: 35 minutes**

**Ingredients:**

- 6 cups of zucchini, shredded
- 2 cups of onion, chopped
- 2 ½ tablespoons of canning salt
- 1 bell pepper, seeded and chopped
- 3 cups of white sugar
- 1 ¼ cups of white vinegar
- ½ tablespoon of cornstarch
- ¾ teaspoon of celery seeds
- ⅓ teaspoon of ground turmeric
- ⅓ teaspoon of ground nutmeg
- ¼ teaspoon of ground black pepper

**Directions:**

1. In a large non-reactive bowl, add chopped zucchini, onion and salt and stir to combine well.
2. Cover the bowl and refrigerate overnight.
3. In a colander, drain the zucchini mixture and rinse well.
4. Again, drain the zucchini mixture completely and then with your hands, squeeze out excess liquid.
5. In a non-reactive saucepan, add the chopped bell peppers, sugar, vinegar, cornstarch and spices and stir to combine.
6. Add the drained zucchini mixture and stir to combine.
7. Place the saucepan over medium-high heat and bring to a boil.
8. Now adjust the heat to medium-low and simmer, uncovered for about 30 minutes.
9. In 7 (½-pint) hot sterilized jars, divide the relish, leaving about ½-inch space from the top.
10. Slide a small knife around the insides of each jar to remove air bubbles.
11. Wipe any trace of food off the rims of jars with a clean, moist kitchen towel.

12. Close each jar with a lid and screw on the ring.
13. Arrange the jars in a boiling water canner and process for about 10 minutes.
14. Remove the jars from water canner and place onto a wood surface several inches apart to cool completely.
15. After cooling with your finger, press the top of each jar's lid to ensure that the seal is tight.
16. The canned relish can be stored in the refrigerator for up to 1 month.

# CHAPTER 14.
# SAUCE RECIPES

## 31. CAYENNE PEPPER SAUCE

**Serving Size: 2 pints**

**Preparation Time: 15 minutes**

**Cooking Time: 25 minutes**

**Ingredients:**

- ⅓ cup of chopped cilantro
- ⅓ cup of minced garlic
- 3 cups of cider vinegar
- 2 ½ cups of water

- 4 cups of sliced onion
- 3 pounds of hot peppers
- 3 cans of diced tomatoes

**Directions:**

1. With a mandolin, slice the onion & peppers into rings.
2. In a pot, add all ingredients. Mix and let it actually come to a boil, boil for 60 minutes.
3. Turn the heat off.
4. Puree with a stick blender. Let it come to a boil. Turn the heat off.
5. In sterilized hot jars, add the mixture, leave half-inch space from above. Remove any air bubbles. Wipe the jar's rim, place the lid on top and screw the bands (do not screw too tightly).
6. Process for 15 minutes.

# 32. Honey Maple Cranberry Sauce

**Serving Size: 2 half-pints**

**Preparation Time: 20 mintues**

**Cooking Time: 30 minutes**

**Ingredients:**

- 2 cups of apple juice
- 1 cinnamon stick
- 1¼ cup of honey
- 1 lemon
- 3 pounds of fresh cranberries
- 1 cup of maple syrup

**Directions:**

1. In a pot, add all ingredients except for lemon juice.
2. Place on a high flame, let it come to a boil. Turn the heat to medium and cook for 15 to 20 minutes.
3. Turn the heat off and let it cool.
4. Take the cinnamon stick. Add lemon juice.
5. In sterilized hot jars, add the mixture, leave half-inch space from above. Remove any air bubbles. Wipe the jar's rim, place the lid on top and screw the bands (do not screw too tightly).
6. Process for 10 minutes.

# 33. Roasted Eggplant and Pepper Puttanesca Sauce

**Serving Size: 6 jars**

**Preparation Time: 10 minutes**

**Cooking Time: 15 minutes**

**Ingredients:**

- 6 lb. plum tomatoes
- Vegetable cooking spray
- 2 pounds of eggplant
- 3 large onions
- 3 red bell peppers
- 2 cups of dry red wine
- 1½ cups of kalamata olives
- 1 tablespoon anchovy paste
- 2 teaspoon salt
- 2 teaspoon dried oregano
- 1 teaspoon black pepper
- 6 garlic cloves
- 1 jar capers

**Directions:**

1. Preheat the oven to a heat of 400°F (200°C). Tomatoes should be peeled and split in half lengthwise. Place tomato halves on two large rimmed baking pans that have been coated with aluminum foil. Bake for approximately about 45 minutes at 400°F (200°C) or until softened and starting to brown. Remove the dish from the oven. Allow cooling completely in the large-sized pan on a wire rack. Peel and roughly chop tomatoes after they have cooled enough to handle. In a 6-qt. stainless steel, combine tomatoes and any collected liquid.
2. Cooking sprays the foil and replaces it on the baking sheets. On one baking sheet, arrange the eggplant; on another, arrange the onion and bell pepper halves. Bake for 30 minutes at a heat of 400°F (200°C) or until eggplant edges are golden brown and onion and bell pepper are crisp-tender.
3. Toss eggplant in with the tomatoes. Remove the skin from the onion and bell pepper and finely chop them before adding them to the tomato mixture. Combine the wine and the other ingredients in a mixing bowl.

4. Bring to a boil, lower to low heat and cook uncovered for 15 minutes. Fill a heated jar halfway with hot sauce, allowing a 12-inch (1-cm) headspace. Air bubbles should be removed. Wipe the jar's rim.
5. On the jar, place the lid in the middle. Apply the band and tighten it until it is fingertip-tight. In a boiling-water canner, place the jar. Rep until all of the jars are full.
6. Adjust for altitude and process the jars for 35 minutes. Remove jars from heat, remove lids, and set aside for 5 minutes. Remove the jars and cool.

# 34. Smokey Bourbon Barbecue Sauce

**Serving Size: 3 pints**

**Preparation Time: 15 minutes**

**Cooking Time: 45 minutes**

**Ingredients:**

- 2 cups of apple cider vinegar
- 6 cups of tomato sauce
- 4 tablespoons of minced garlic
- 1 ½ cups of brown sugar
- 1 ½ cups of chopped onion
- ¾ cup of each tomato paste & Worcestershire sauce
- 1 tablespoon of liquid smoke
- 1 ½ teaspoon of black pepper
- 2 tablespoons of smoked paprika
- 2 ¼ cups of bourbon whiskey
- 1 tablespoon of hot sauce
- 1 to 2 tablespoons of salt (it is optional)

**Directions:**

1. In a pan, add whiskey, onion and garlic. Simmer for ten minutes.
2. Add the rest of the ingredients. Let it actually come to a boil, simmer for 20 minutes.
3. In sterilized hot jars, add the mixture, leave half-inch space from above. Remove any air bubbles. Wipe the jar's rim, place the lid on top and screw the bands (do not screw too tightly).
4. Process the jars for 20 minutes.

# 35. Tangy Cranberry Sauce

**Serving Size: 6-pint jars**

**Preparation Time: 10 minutes**

**Cooking Time: 15 minutes**

**Ingredients:**

- 4 (12-ounces / 340-g) bags fresh cranberries (8 cups)
- 2 cups sugar
- 2 cups water
- 2 cups bottled orange juice
- 2 large oranges, peeled, pith removed, seeded, and chopped
- ½ teaspoon ground allspice (optional)
- ½ teaspoon ground cloves (optional)

**Directions:**

1. In a smaller pot, attach lids and rings, 1 tbsp. distilled white vinegar, and water to cover. Boil for 5 minutes, then detach from heat.
2. In a large pot, combine the cranberries, sugar, water, orange juice, oranges, allspice, and cloves. Set to a boil over medium-high heat, stirring often. Set the heat to a heat of low and simmer for 15 minutes. Stir often, muddling the orange pieces with your spoon. Remove from heat.
3. Set the hot jars on a cutting board. Using a funnel, ladle the hot sauce into the jars, leaving a 1/2-inch headspace. Detach any air bubbles and add additional sauce, if necessary, to maintain the 1/2-inch headspace.
4. Clean the jar with a warm washcloth dipped in distilled white vinegar. Set a lid and ring on each jar and hand-tighten.
5. Bring the jars in the water bather, ensuring each jar is covered by at least 1 inch of water. Attach 2 tablespoons distilled white vinegar to the water and turn the heat to high. Set the canner to a boil and process both quarts and pints for 15 minutes. When processed, wait 5 minutes before removing the jars from the canner.

# CHAPTER 15.
# SALSA RECIPES

## 36. BEAN AND PINEAPPLE SALSA

**Serving Size: 8 pints**

**Preparation Time: 20 minutes**

**Cooking Time: 0 minutes**

**Ingredients:**

- 1 cup of chopped pineapple
- 2 peppers green chile peppers, diced
- ¼ cup of chopped onions
- 15 ounces of black beans

- 1 cup of frozen corn kernels
- ½ cup of diced green bell pepper
- ½ cup of diced red bell pepper
- ¼ cup of orange juice
- ¼ cup of chopped fresh cilantro
- ½ teaspoon of ground cumin
- 1 pinch of salt
- 1 pinch of pepper

**Directions:**

1. Set together all the ingredients in a large bowl and season with salt, cumin, and pepper.
2. Transfer to a container and seal tightly.
3. Store in the fridge until chilled before serving.

# 37. Corn Avocado Salsa

**Serving Size: 10 half-pint jars**

**Preparation Time: 30 minutes**

**Cooking Time: 0 minutes**

**Ingredients:**

- 4 avocados, diced
- 2 cups of frozen corn kernels, thawed
- 1 small onion, chopped
- 1 red bell pepper, chopped
- ½ cup of sliced ripe olives, drained
- 1 teaspoon of dried oregano
- 5 cloves of garlic, minced
- 3 tablespoons of cider vinegar
- ¼ cup of lemon juice
- ⅓ cup of olive oil
- ½ teaspoon of salt
- ½ teaspoon of pepper

**Directions:**

1. In a bowl, combine onion, red bell pepper, olives, and corn.
2. In a small bowl, set together apple cider vinegar, lemon juice, olive oil, oregano, garlic, salt, and pepper until well merged; pour into the corn mixture and toss until well coated. Transfer to sterile jars or cans and seal. Refrigerate until ready to serve.

# 38. Fresh Green Salsa

**Serving Size: 12-pint jars**

**Preparation Time: 10 minutes**

**Cooking Time: 30 minutes**

**Ingredients:**

- 2 jalapeno peppers, diced
- 6 green onions, sliced
- 7 cups of tomatoes, diced
- 4 cloves of garlic, minced
- 2 tablespoons of minced cilantro
- 4 drops of hot pepper sauce
- 2 tablespoons of lime juice
- ½ cup of vinegar
- 2 teaspoons of salt

**Directions:**

1. Merge all ingredients in a pan, set to a boil, and then simmer for 15 minutes. Ladle in sterile jars and seal.
2. Bring a hot water bath for about 15 minutes and then let cool before storing in the fridge.

# 39. Mild Jalapeno Tomato Salsa

**Serving Size: 10 pints**

**Preparation Time: 40 minutes**

**Cooking Time: 20 minutes**

**Ingredients:**

- 10 ½ pounds of tomatoes, peeled, quartered
- 3 large onions, chopped
- 4 medium green peppers, chopped
- 1 medium sweet red pepper, chopped
- 1 celery rib, chopped
- 4 jalapeno peppers, seeded, chopped
- 24 ounces of tomato paste
- ¼ teaspoon of hot pepper sauce
- 13/4 cups of white vinegar
- ½ cup of sugar
- 15 garlic cloves, minced
- ¼ cup of canning salt

**Directions:**

1. In a large stockpot, cook tomatoes over medium heat, 20 minutes, uncovered. Drain, reserving 2 cups liquid. Return tomatoes to the pot.
2. Add remaining ingredients and the reserved tomato liquid. Bring to a boil. Reduce heat and let simmer for 1 hour, frequently stirring, uncovered.
3. Scoop the hot mixture in hot sterilized 1-pint jars, leaving 1/4-inch space of the top. Remove any air bubbles and adjust headspace as needed by adding hot mixture. Wipe the rims with a soft cloth. Screw on bands until fingertip tight. Place caps on jars and screw on bands until fingertip tight.
4. Set jars into a canner, ensuring that they are completely covered with water. Let boil for 20 minutes. Remove jars and cool.

## 40. ZESTY SALSA

**Serving Size: 6 pints**

**Preparation Time: 1 hour**

**Cooking Time: 5 minutes**

**Ingredients:**

- 10 cups of tomatoes, chopped
- 5 cups of bell peppers, chopped
- 5 cups of onions, chopped
- 2 ½ cups of hot peppers, chopped
- 1 ¼ cup of cider vinegar
- 3 cloves of garlic, minced
- 2 tablespoons of cilantro, minced
- 3 teaspoons of salt
- 1 can of tomato paste

**Directions:**

1. In a large saucepan, combine all ingredients except the tomato paste.
2. Simmer for approximately three minutes or until the sauce has thickened.
3. Add the tomato paste and stir to combine.
4. Ladle the hot salsa into jars, allowing a headspace of approximately 14 inches.
5. Place the jars in a warm water bath for 15 minutes.
6. Allow cooling fully before storing in an airtight container.

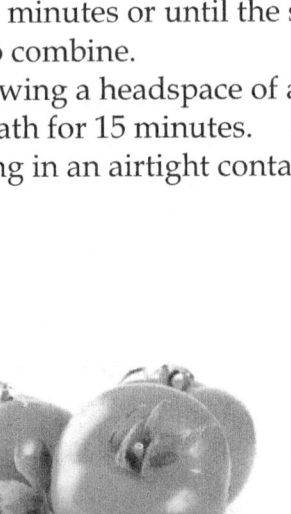

# Chapter 16.
# Vegetable Recipes

## 41. Asparagus Pickle

**Serving Size: 14**

**Preparation Time: 20 minutes**

**Cooking Time: 10 minutes**

**Ingredients:**

- 6-7 pound of asparagus tips, trimmed
- 5 cups of white vinegar
- 5 cups of water
- 1 ¼ cups of white sugar

- 7 tablespoons of kosher salt
- 8 teaspoons of red pepper flakes, crushed
- 8 teaspoons of dill seed
- 8 whole garlic cloves, peeled and each cut into 3 slices
- 1 jalapeño pepper, cut into slices

**Directions:**

1. In a large-sized saucepan of boiling water, add the asparagus and again bring to a boil.
2. Immediately drain the asparagus and transfer into a bowl of ice water to cool.
3. Drain the asparagus well and pat dry with a paper towel.
4. In a medium-sized saucepan, add vinegar, water, sugar, and salt and bring to a boil, stirring continuously.
5. Meanwhile, divide the red pepper flakes, dill seed, and garlic cloves into 4 (1-quart) hot sterilized jars evenly.
6. Then divide the blanched asparagus into jars.
7. Pour the vinegar over the asparagus, leaving about ¼-½-inch space from the top.
8. Slide a small knife around the insides of each jar to remove air bubbles.
9. Wipe any trace of food off the rims of jars with a clean, moist kitchen towel.
10. Close each jar with a lid and screw on the ring.
11. Arrange the jars in a boiling water canner and process for about 10 minutes.
12. Remove the jars from water canner and place onto a wood surface several inches apart to cool completely.
13. After cooling with your finger, press the top of each jar's lid to ensure that the seal is tight.
14. Place the jars of pickle in refrigerator for up to 1 month.

# 42. Asparagus Spear

**Serving Size: 9 pints**

**Preparation Time: 15 minutes**

**Cooking Time: 30 minutes**

**Ingredients:**

- 16 pounds asparagus spears
- 10 tablespoons of salt
- boiling water

**Directions:**

1. In a large pot, cover the asparagus with boiling water and add salt. Boil for 3 minutes. Fill the sterilized jars loosely with the asparagus and liquid, leaving 1-inch headspace.
2. Adjust the jar lids and process the jars for 30 minutes in a pressure canner.

# 43. Cabbage and Bell Pepper Pickle

**Serving Size: 12**

**Preparation Time: 15 minutes**

**Cooking Time: 5 minutes**

**Ingredients:**

- 2 pounds of cabbage, cored and shredded
- 5 cups of bell peppers, seeded and cut into thin strips
- ¼ cup of pickling salt
- 1 ½ cup of white wine vinegar
- 1 cup of white sugar
- 6 garlic cloves, minced
- 4 teaspoons of mustard seeds
- ½ teaspoon of hot pepper flakes

**Directions:**

1. In a glass bowl, add cabbage, bell peppers and salt and mix well.
2. Cover the glass bowl and place in a cool place for about 8-12 hours.
3. Rinse the cabbage and drain completely.
4. In the bowl of cabbage mixture, add the garlic, mustard seeds and red pepper flakes and toss to coat well.
5. In a non-reactive saucepan, add the vinegar and sugar and bring to a boil.
6. In the bottom of 4 (1-pint) hot sterilized jars, divide the cabbage mixture.
7. Pour the hot vinegar mixture over the cabbage mixture, leaving about ½-inch space from the top.
8. Slide a small knife around the insides of each jar to remove air bubbles.
9. Wipe any trace of food off the rims of jars with a clean, moist kitchen towel.
10. Close each jar with a lid and screw on the ring.
11. Arrange the jars in a boiling water canner and process for about 10 minutes.
12. Remove the jars from water canner and place onto a wood surface several inches apart to cool completely.
13. After cooling with your finger, press the top of each jar's lid to ensure that the seal is tight.
14. Place the jars of pickle in refrigerator for up to 1 month.

# 44. CUCUMBER SLICES

**Serving Size: 5 pints**

**Preparation Time: 40 minutes**

**Cooking Time: 20 minutes**

**Ingredients:**

- 3 ½ pound of pickling cucumbers
- 4 cups cider vinegar
- 3 cups Splenda
- 1 tablespoon canning salt
- 1 cup water
- 1 tablespoon mustard seed
- 1 tablespoon whole allspice
- 1 tablespoon celery seed
- 4 1-inch cinnamon sticks

**Directions:**

1. Wash the prepared cucumbers and cut off the blossom end. Discard. Cut the cucumbers into ¼-inch pieces thickness then pour boiling water over them. Let stand for 10 minutes.
2. Drain the hot water and pour running cold water on the cucumbers. Drain the cucumber slices thoroughly.
3. Mix all other ingredients except cinnamon sticks in a stockpot and bring to boil. Add the cucumber slices and return to boil.
4. Place a cinnamon stick in each sterilized jar then using a slotted spoon, fill the jars with the hot cucumber pieces leaving a ½-inch headspace.
5. Remove any air bubbles then wipe the rims with a clean damp paper towel. Process the jars in the pressure canner at 10 pounds pressure for 10 minutes.

# 45. DILL PICKLE SPEARS

**Serving Size: 7 pints**

**Preparation Time: 20 minutes**

**Cooking Time: 30 minutes**

**Ingredients:**

- 2 gallons water
- ½ cup pickling salt
- 8 pounds pickling cucumbers, quartered lengthwise
- ½ cup mustard seeds
- 24 fresh dill sprigs
- 6 garlic cloves, halved
- 1 ½ quarts white vinegar
- 4 cups water
- ¼ cup sugar
- 2 tablespoons of Pickling spice

**Directions:**

1. Combine the prepared water and salt in a large pot, stirring to dissolve the salt. Add the cucumbers and let it stand at room temperature for 12 hours.
2. Place 2 teaspoons of the mustard seeds, 2 of the dill sprigs, and 1 of the garlic cloves halves in each sterilized jar. Drain the cucumbers and divide them among the jars.
3. Mix together the vinegar, 4 cups of water, the sugar, and the pickling spice in a large saucepan. Bring the pot to a boil and cook for 10 minutes. Pour the hot vinegar mixture into the jars, filling to ½-inch from top. Clean the prepared jar rims and add the lids to the jars. Process these in a prepared boiling water bath for 20 minutes.

# 46. Dilled Green Tomatoes

**Serving Size: 4 pints**

**Preparation Time: 20 minutes**

**Cooking Time: 15 minutes**

**Ingredients:**

- 1 clove garlic
- 1 stalk celery
- 1 hot green pepper
- 1 head of dill
- Salt
- Green tomatoes

**Directions:**

1. Pack clean, small, green tomatoes (stems left on) into hot, sterile quart jars.
2. Place all ingredients to the jars
3. Combine 2 quarts water, 1-quart apple cider vinegar, and 1 cup pickling (kosher) salt.
4. Bring to a boil.
5. Fill jars with liquid, leaving 1″ head space.
6. Process prepared jars in a boiling water bath for fifteen minutes.

# 47. Eggplant Pickle

**Serving Size: 6 pints**

**Preparation Time: 35 minutes**

**Cooking Time: 10 minutes**

**Ingredients:**

- 4 ½ cups of cold water
- Half cup of balsamic vinegar
- 2 teaspoons of Pickling salt
- 6 cloves garlic
- 3 tablespoons of granulated sugar
- 1 ½ cups of white vinegar
- 5 pounds of eggplant
- 1 tablespoon of oregano leaves

**Directions:**

1. In a pot, add water and boil. Peel the prepared eggplant and cut it into 3" long strips (¾" wide). Add to the boiling water, keep them submerged under hot water, cook until tender. Transfer to cold water.
2. Drain and pat dry. Add the rest of the ingredients (except for the garlic) to a pot. Let it come to a boil until sugar dissolves. Turn the heat off.
3. In each sterilized jar, add garlic cloves with eggplant and pour hot liquid on top; leave half-inch space from above. Remove any air bubbles. Wipe the jar's rim, place the lid on top and screw the bands (do not screw too tightly). Boil for 15 minutes.
4. Take the jars out and cool for 12 to 24 hours, and the lid should not pop down or up. Store in a cool, dark place.

# 48. PICKLED SQUASH

**Serving Size: 15**

**Preparation Time: 4 hours**

**Cooking Time: 15 minutes**

**Ingredients:**

- ¼ cup salt
- 2 ½ pounds young yellow squash and zucchini, sliced into rounds
- 1 green bell pepper, small strips
- 2 small onions, thinly sliced
- 2 ¼ cups white sugar
- 2 cups distilled white vinegar
- 2 teaspoons mustard seed
- 1 teaspoon ground turmeric
- 1 teaspoon celery seed

**Directions:**

1. Put onion, bell pepper and squash in big non-aluminum pot; cover with salt. Let stand to release liquids for 2 hours; occasionally mix.
2. Right before 2 hours finish, mix celery seed, turmeric, mustard seed, vinegar and sugar in saucepan; boil. Drain salty liquid from veggies. Put spice brine on veggies; let stand for 2 hours more.
3. Boil again; simmer for 5 minutes. Put in 1-pint. Sterile jars to fill with liquid to within ¼ -in. of top. Use clean towel to wipe rims; use a thin spatula to run around inside of jar to get rid of air bubbles. Use lids and rings to seal. Process in prepared simmering water bath for 10 minutes to completely seal.

# 49. PUMPKIN BUTTER

**Serving Size: 2 jars**

**Preparation Time: 15 minutes**

**Cooking Time: 20 minutes**

**Ingredients:**

- 1 (29 ounce) can of solid pack pumpkin puree
- 1 tablespoon of pumpkin pie spice
- 1 (2 ounce) package of dry pectin
- 4 ½ cups white sugar

**Directions:**

1. In a medium saucepan, mix the solid pack pumpkin puree, dry pectin, and pumpkin pie spice over high heat. Bring the mixture to a boil. Stir in sugar, adding it all at once.
2. Whisk the mixture often until it returns to a full boil. Boil the mixture for a minute. Remove it from the preheated heat and pour it immediately into the sterile containers. Seal the containers and let them chill inside the fridge until serving.

# 50. WHOLE TOMATOES

**Serving Size: 7-pint jars**

**Preparation Time: 20 minutes**

**Cooking Time: 35 minutes**

**Ingredients:**

- 85–90 medium tomatoes
- Water, about 10 cups
- 1 cup commercially bottled lemon juice
- 2 ½ tablespoons salt

**Directions:**

1. The tomatoes should be washed and peeled before being cored and placed in a big saucepan. Cook for 5 minutes on low heat, covered with water. Add lemon juice and 12 teaspoons salt in each container Toss whole (or half-cut) tomatoes into jars. Spoon hot cooking water into a 12-inch headspace and over them.
2. Process after popping the bubbles, wiping the rims, and placing the lids on top. Before peeling tomatoes, they are blanched. You'll need a pot of boiling water and ice water. Using a colander or strainer, drop some tomatoes into the boiling water. Count to 60 slowly before plunging the colander into the icy water for 60 seconds.
3. The skins of the tomatoes should be split and peeled. Because the tomatoes may still be hot, gloves should be used to remove the skins. In the bottom of each jar, measure out the salt and lemon juice. They'll be spread throughout the jar after they've been treated. Using a slotted spoon, lift the tomatoes. Fill jars to the top without squeezing the tomatoes.
4. The tomatoes in the jars are spooned with cooking water. Create bubbles using a bubble stick, then add additional fluid as required. Bring some additional water to a boil and cover the tomatoes if you run out of cooking water.

# CHAPTER 17.
# FAQS ON CANNING AND PRESERVING FOODS

This book has tried to cover all areas that a beginner or newbie in canning and preserving food would want to know. Nevertheless, there may still be some questions that are hanging in your mind. Here are the most frequently asked questions and their answers regarding canning and preserving foods.

**As an interested beginner who would like to take this skill into a higher level, is there a canning class or course that one can take?**

Anybody can preserve or can foods without formal education. For those who would like to have advanced canning skills, canning classes are oftentimes offered in some grocery stores, kitchen stores, cooking schools, community centers, and sometimes, even in libraries. You could also search online for correspondence that offers this course. Be careful with blogs or articles that teach canning techniques. Some of these articles may contain ideas or suggestions that go contrary to the recommendations of USDA. If in doubt, refer to the USDA manual or contact an authorized person.

## What is the Shelf Life of Preserved Canned Food?

Properly sealed canned and preserved foods placed in a cool, dry place, with no signs of spoilage inside and out, are considered safe to consume for at least a year. However, canned foods stored near a furnace, in indirect sunlight, a range or anywhere warm can decrease shelf life. It would be safe to consume within a few weeks until a couple of months only. Placing the jars or cans in damp areas may corrode cans and this can cause leakage, causing the food to be contaminated and unsafe to eat.

## Can you process two layers of jars at one time?

Yes, this can be done. The jars at the upper layer would enjoy the same benefits as those in the bottom. The temperature is equally distributed making it safe for all jars, whether in the upper and lower layer. Just make sure that you place a wire rack between the layers to allow the circulation of water and steam around the jars. Also, when using bath-water canning method, make sure that the water is up to one inch above the tops of the jars in the upper layer. As always, comply with the processing time and required temperature.

## During processing, some liquid of the contents was lost. What should be done about it?

The food will not spoil, and the seal will not be affected. It may cause slight discoloration of the food, however, but that's about it. However, if the liquid loss is at least half of the original amount, then the most that you can do is to refrigerate it and consume within 2 to 3 days.

## What is kettle canning and is this safe to use?

In this method, the foods to be preserved are cooked in an ordinary household kettle. After that, the foods are placed into hot jars, covered, and sealed. You would notice that no processing is done in this method. In addition, the temperature when using the kettle canning method is not high enough to eliminate the harmful bacteria that may be in the food. Also, during the transfer of food from the kettle to the jars, microorganisms can enter the food and cause spoilage and worse, food poisoning, later on. Therefore, the safety of food is not guaranteed. The kettle canning method is not included in the recommendation of USDA with regards to canning.

**Why do some jars break during canning?**

There are many reasons breakage occurs during the process of canning. Here are five reasons:

The glass of the jar is not tempered. A tempered or toughened glass underwent a process that increased its strength and ability to withstand heat compared to normal glass. Before buying commercial food jars, make sure that they are manufactured for home canning.

Another reason is using jars with hairline cracks. These cracks are so thin that they can be missed or overlooked. Such jars would not be able to stand the extreme heat during processing time.

Not placing a wire rack on the bottom of the pot or canner could also cause the jars to break.

Putting newly cooked food into cold jars. The difference in the temperature between the food and the jars could lead to breakage. That is why it is advised that the jars should be maintained on a hot temperature before filling them with hot food.

Jars with unheated or raw food placed directly into boiling water can also break because of the sudden change in temperature. It is better to use hot water first and let it achieve boiling point after several minutes.

Molds can cause an increase in the pH of the food. For instance, if the canned food is high acid, then because of the raised pH, it could become low acid. This places the preserved food into the risk of having botulism and other bacterial growth. Therefore, all canned foods with molds should be disposed of properly. Follow the proper waste disposal for spoiled canned food.

**Can canning be done for those people with special diets?**

Some people, because of their medical conditions, would not be allowed to consume some of the canned foods because of some ingredients like sugar and salt. Sugar is discouraged among diabetic people due to the effect of increased blood sugar with the intake of simple sugar.

On the other hand, salts are always restricted among people with cardiovascular disorders as this can cause increased high blood pressure as more body water is retained because of salts. Still, canning foods can be done for these people even in the absence of salt or sugar. However, the color, texture, flavor of these canned foods will differ from those with sugar or salt in them, as expected. Other people find these special diet canned foods to be less acceptable and less appealing.

To can vegetables, meats, seafood, or tomatoes without salt, proceed with the regular canning minus the salt. This method is allowed, as salts are not considered as preservatives, hence the safety of food is still guaranteed even in the absence of salt. Salt substitutes can be offered upon serving to make the preserved food taste better.

**What is the future of canning and preserving foods?**

The trend all over the world right now is towards healthy food and lifestyle. You can see everything "organic" from cosmetics, hair products, food, baby products, and even processed foods. People prefer "fresh" than canned or commercially prepared processed foods.

This is where home canning and preserving fresh fruits, meats, poultry, salsa, vegetables, sauces, and what-have-you enter the picture. This is a combination of being healthy and modern, rolled into one. It meets the requirements of being healthy and at the same time, lasting longer on the shelf or pantry. It is ready to eat, answering the need for convenience and saving precious time.

More and more people are going into canning and preserving food. The threat of not having enough good food to eat in the future due to excessive wasting and unnecessary throwing of food today has found its solution in canning.

# CONCLUSION

You might be feeling a little overwhelmed after reading all of this. Don't be alarmed; this is completely normal. Don't be daunted by a large amount of information. This book was not written to frighten you or make you feel inept. No. If anything, this book was written to help you navigate the difficulties that home canning may present.

Canning your own food is a gratifying hobby. When you look at your canned foods and realize you were able to do it on your own, it will provide you with the motivation you need to make this a regular habit. If you regularly can your own food, you will notice a decrease in the amount of money you spend on produce and other canned foods. Home canning will also have a positive impact on your eating habits. The foods that you will preserve will be far healthier than the preserved foods sold in supermarkets.

Once you've mastered the art of canning your own food, you'll be unstoppable! I won't lie to you and tell you that everything will be simple – especially the first few times.

However, as time passes, the number of errors you make will decrease, and you will no longer require the assistance of this guide. You will be able to create your own unique recipes! This has to begin with the first steps, the first steps being that you are giving this a shot.

Made in the USA
Las Vegas, NV
14 August 2023

76091145R00142